Founded in 1972, the Institute for Research on Public policy is an independent, national, nonprofit organization. Its mission is to improve public policy in Canada by promoting and contributing to a policy process that is more broadly based, informed and effective.

In pursuit of this mission, the IRPP

■ identifies significant public policy questions that will confront Canada in the longer term future and undertakes independent research into these questions;

■ promotes wide dissemination of key results from its own and other research activities;

■ encourages non-partisan discussion and criticism of public policy issues by eliciting broad participation from all sectors and regions of Canadian society and linking research with processes of social learning and policy formation.

The IRPP's independence is assured by an endowment fund, to which federal and provincial governments and the private sector have contributed.

INSTITUTE FOR RESEARCH ON PUBLIC POLICY

iRPP

INSTITUT DE RECHERCHE EN POLITIQUES PUBLIQUES

Créé en 1972, l'Institut de recherche en politiques publiques est un organisme national et indépendant à but non lucratif.

L'IRPP a pour mission de favoriser le développement de la pensée politique au Canada par son appui et son apport à un processus élargi, plus éclairé et plus efficace d'élaboration et d'expression des politiques publiques.

Dans le cadre de cette mission, l'IRPP a pour mandat :

- d'identifier les questions politiques auxquelles le Canada sera confronté dans l'avenir et d'entreprendre des recherches indépendantes à leur sujet;
- de favoriser une large diffusion des résultats les plus importants de ses propres recherches et de celles des autres sur ces questions;
- de promouvoir une analyse et une discussion objectives des questions politiques de manière à faire participer activement au débat public tous les secteurs de la société canadienne et toutes les régions du pays, et à rattacher la recherche à l'évolution sociale et à l'élaboration de politiques.

L'indépendance de l'IRPP est assurée par les revenus d'un fonds de dotation auquel ont souscrit les gouvernements fédéral et provinciaux, ainsi que le secteur privé.

INSTITUTE FOR RESEARCH ON PUBLIC POLICY

IRPP

INSTITUT DE RECHERCHE EN POLITIQUES PUBLIQUES

Rethinking Government:

Reform or Reinvention?

F. Leslie Seidle, Editor

Copyright © The Institute for Research on Public Policy (IRPP) 1993
All rights reserved

Printed in Canada

Bibliothèque nationale du Québec
Dépôt légal 1993

Canadian Cataloguing in Publication Data

Main entry under title:
Rethinking Government : Reform or Reinvention?

Proceedings of a roundtable held in Montreal on 11th June 1993

ISBN 0-88645-151-5

1. Administrative agencies—Reorganization. 2. Public administration. 3. Local government. 4. Organizational change. I. Seidle, F. Leslie II. Institute for Research on Public
Policy.

JL81.R48 1993   320.4   C93-090615-2

Director of Publications, IRPP
Marye Bos
_____

Editor
F. Leslie Seidle

Copy Editor
Mathew Horsman

Design and Production
Schumacher Design

Cover Illustration
Jacques Cournoyer

Published by
The Institute for Research on Public Policy (IRPP)
L'Institut de recherche en politiques publiques
1470 Peel Street, Suite 200
Montreal, Quebec H3A 1T1

Distributed by
Renouf Publishing Co. Ltd.
1294 Algoma Road
Ottawa, Ontario K1B 3W8
For orders, call 613-741-4333

FOREWORD

As we approach the end of the century, our current methods of governance are being increasingly questioned. The forces of globalization are expanding our horizons, the role of the nation-state is in flux and the search for a sense of community is ever growing. We can no longer rely on our traditional reference points. This is especially true regarding the future shape of government and its responsibilities. Indeed, along with many other countries, Canada is launched on a process of rethinking government.

This process will be more fundamental than past attempts at reform. It will go far beyond approaches such as "total quality management" and "cultural change," which focus primarily on government processes. Rethinking government means taking a hard look at the size and structure of the public service, particularly in the light of the perilous state of public finances. It means dispelling the common belief that a public good is a free good. Rethinking government also means devising ways of responding to the needs of citizens, who increasingly demand that services from the public and private sectors be of comparable quality. Significant reform is required to close the gap.

As part of its examination of these issues, IRPP sponsored a roundtable, "Rethinking Government: Reform or Reinvention?" in June 1993. The event brought together distinguished members of the Canadian and international communities. Stimulating presentations by Ted Gaebler, co-author of *Reinventing Government,* and Bill Jenkins, a leading British academic authority, allowed participants to learn about major innovations elsewhere. Three Canadian scholars presented insightful papers on important aspects of these issues. The papers and other proceedings of the roundtable are published here.

3

The IRPP roundtable proved to be a timely initiative. Two weeks later, a new federal Cabinet was named, with 25 ministers (compared to 35 immediately before); a restructuring reduced the number of federal departments from 32 to 23. Rationalization of the organization of these departments is proceeding. These are only first steps, however, on the path to genuine reform.

The current rethinking of government is not a fad. The transformation of government administration that lies ahead is inevitable and irreversible. A process has been launched, but much remains to be done. We hope this volume will contribute in a significant way to the well-informed and broad debate so necessary to advancing that process.

Monique Jérôme-Forget, President
IRPP

CONTENTS

INTRODUCTION

The present lack of confidence in how Canada is governed encompasses not only elected institutions but also the administrative (public service) sector. The past decade has seen reforms such as deregulation and privatization, as well as the Public Service 2000 initiative. The latter led to some simplification of management structures (e.g., delayering), moves to "empower" managers and employees,[1] and efforts to build bridges with various groups through "partnerships."[2] It has become increasingly clear, however, that such reforms are, at best, a partial answer.[3]

The need for more fundamental change was implicit in the restructuring of the federal public service launched in mid-1993. While this responds in part to public concern about the cost and complexity of government, other factors that are undermining confidence in government and its role in Canadian society have been less examined, among them that government administration does not pay sufficient attention to the quality of service, is not judged on the basis of results,[4] and does not allow for adequate client and public involvement in the development and implementation of policies.

A growing view — though not without dissenters — is that public service institutions must be redefined or even "reinvented." In *Reinventing Government*,[5] David Osborne and Ted Gaebler argue that public service management is better suited to steering (catalyzing and facilitating action) than rowing (undue focus on the actual delivery of service). In their view, what is needed is "entrepreneurial government": public sector institutions should anticipate problems rather than simply react to them, encourage competition (thus expanding consumer choice), and measure and publicize results.

IRPP decided to tap this emerging interest in alternative approaches to administrative reform by sponsoring a roundtable on "Rethinking Government: Reform or Reinvention?" Consistent with our view that a broad perspective was required, we cast our sights not only south of the border but across the Atlantic, where major reform of the British civil service was well under way (though little noticed by Canadian commentators). We also felt it important to examine local government as a potential laboratory for new approaches[6] and to consider the relations between governments and citizens. The results of this exploration are found in this volume: two presentations by Ted Gaebler, four papers by leading academic authorities and, for each of the papers, the comments of a discussant.

As this book went to press, the National Performance Review chaired by US Vice President Gore issued its report calling for reinvention of the American federal administration. While sceptics suggested various interests would soon erect roadblocks,[7] there was no doubt that the call for innovation in American government had moved from concept to credo. In Canada, it seemed clear that — whatever the outcome of the election then in progress — a process of rethinking the federal government would continue, extending beyond the usual preoccupation with adjusting structures and internal procedures.[8] We hope that the research and discussion on these issues sponsored by IRPP will further advance this debate.

In opening the roundtable, IRPP President Monique Jérôme-Forget expressed the view that "internal tinkering" in relation to government administration at various levels will no longer suffice; rather, rethinking what we have taken for "government" is required. She suggested this process should include an examination of: the size and structure of government; how governments work, particularly how decisions are taken and how government organizations are managed; and how government relates to and serves citizens. She called on Canada's political leadership to provide a vision for reform and to support the ensuing process.

In the first of two interventions, Ted Gaebler stresses the role of information — correct or otherwise — in influencing perceptions about government. He provides statistics on the scale of government and public spending in the US and other Western countries. He predicts a transformation of the role and mission of government due to competition with other organizations for the provision of services, changing citizen expectations about the quality of services and the need to re-work "archaic, centralized" internal systems. Gaebler further amplified his call for the reinvention of government during the luncheon address; readers interested in learning more about his diagnosis and prescription may wish to consult the companion text, "Reinventing Government: Priorities and Potential."

Paul Thomas presented the first paper, "Coping with Change: How Public and Private Organizations Read and Respond to Turbulent External Environments." Thomas and his colleague Benjamin Levin have been studying how four organizations (three in the public sector and one in the private sector) respond to changes in the environments in which they function. Thomas reports here that: the private-sector organization had a more refined strategic planning process and stronger central control than the public-sector organizations; for both types of organization, urgent operational matters and crisis management tend to limit the impact of strategic planning; and, more generally, that public-sector organizations face greater challenges in managing change than private-sector organizations because the environments of the former are more complicated and interconnected. The paper includes an extensive review of recent literature on organizational environments and organizational change, particularly in the private sector.

Sandford Borins, the discussant for Thomas' paper, notes that the research confirms a growing recognition that the public sector consists of organizations and that progress can result from applying the "insights" of those who have systematically studied organizations. Borins suggests certain environmental trends are having an impact on both public- and private-sector organizations, among them the effect of information technology on the nature of jobs and organizational structure, and pressures from global competition and public sector debt burden that demand more efficient budgeting and human resources practices. Discussion among roundtable participants followed Borins' comments; a summary is included (as is the case for the other three sessions).

The roundtable's comparative perspective was reflected further in the paper "Reshaping the Management of Government: The Next Steps Initiative in the United Kingdom," by Bill Jenkins and Andrew Gray. The paper provides a comprehensive review of the major transformation occurring in the UK under the Next Steps program. Key objectives of this initiative have been to separate responsibilities for policy development and delivery of services through the creation of "executive agencies," and to foster a more businesslike and client-oriented approach to service delivery in the operation of these agencies. While the authors suggest Next Steps has succeeded as a management innovation, they believe it is premature to judge the impact of elements such as performance targets and contracting out. Jenkins and Gray raise important questions about the implications of the "federalized administrative structure" that may be emerging.

Louis Bernard, the discussant for this session, refers to what has been achieved under the Next Steps program as a "considerable feat," and underlines the importance of a "high level of political clout" in carrying forward such changes. On the potential for significant government management reform in Quebec, Bernard said the need is there, but so far not the will, and attributes this to the opposition of senior ministers to moves that would "tamper with a strict application of the rule of absolute ministerial responsibility." Commenting on managerial reform in general, Bernard cautions against expecting too much from administrative reform and concludes that enhancement of the democratic process is essential to improving the development of public policy.

Ted Gaebler was the keynote speaker during the luncheon. In "Reinventing Government: Priorities and Potential," he argues that, for at least the next decade, the American public will be unwilling to allocate greater resources to government. While this constitutes a major factor leading to change, Gaebler suggests that the lesson from past unsuccessful efforts (some of which he documents) is that a true transformation will only occur if led by those who work in government — by empowering them and changing the incentives for their behaviour. Finally, Gaebler makes the case for government to become "catalytic" — less involved in the direct delivery of services and more focussed on how to "meld, merge and match" all of society's resources.

Liora Salter's paper, "Experiencing a Sea Change in the Democratic Potential of Regulation," explores a model for examining democracy in regulation, viewing regulation as a form of governance. She focuses on four elements — co-management, direct democracy, due process and delegated legislation — to assess how they each support and at the same time potentially undermine the democratic potential in regulation. Drawing on the analysis of "keywords" in this domain, Salter concludes that in the last decade this potential has been curtailed. She argues for combining all four elements because each offers the possibility of off-setting some of the negative consequences of the others.

Susan Phillips, commenting on Salter's paper, argues that significant limitations on who participates in the regulatory process and the nature of their participation derive from the nature of knowledge demanded by the process. While some interveners have the resources to produce expert information and "act in institutional ways," Phillips observes that others — notably social movements — are less well-placed to do so and/or devote energy to more political activities. She suggests there is a strong case for providing financial and other support to less well advantaged groups to allow their participation in policy formulation and ensure representation of "the diversity of society."

David Siegel presented the final paper of the roundtable. He suggests local governments should be potentially fruitful "laboratories to test innovations," not least because of their proximity to citizens. According to Siegel, this potential has not yet been realized because provincial governments often limit the scope of municipal decision making, diversity within municipal associations limits their capacity for collective action and municipal managers are not sufficiently comfortable with innovating. Among Siegel's recommendations are that there should be less detailed provincial government control, and that local government managers receive appropriate experience and training so they will be better qualified as chief administrative officers.

Jacques Léveillée agrees with David Siegel's conclusion that there must be a more flexible relationship between municipalities and the provincial government, although he expresses the view that new responsibilities should not be transferred to municipalities "without restraints." Léveillée discusses ways in which the Ville de Montréal has expanded training for its managers, reduced hierarchy, delegated power to managers close to daily operations and made services more accessible. He concludes with a brief account of how, in the field of recreation, the city has developed partnerships with some 2,300 organizations.

As rapporteur, I concluded that a "keyword" in the day's proceedings was "change." Participants seemed to agree that, in charting a course, the perspective should be broad; reforms of other government institutions need to be considered, along with the links among them. Factors to bear in mind in fostering a true transformation are the need for a clear plan and political leadership, how to make the best use of revenues and human resources, and the potential for improving service to citizens. Taking all this into account, I suggest that the task ahead is, essentially, "reinventing governance."

IRPP's "rethinking government" project, conceived in early 1993, was a partnership which involved consultation with and support from a number of sectors (see Acknowledgements). We are most grateful to all those who assisted us in organizing the roundtable. Similarly, production of this volume has been a collegial process. I wish to thank the authors whose work appears here for their willingness to explore issues we wanted to bring to the fore and their cooperation in meeting deadlines. At IRPP, I received valued support from Siobhan Harty, Marye Bos, Michel Poulin, Louise Dubuc and Mathew Horsman, who, as copy-editor, demonstrated that effectiveness and congeniality are not incompatible. Finally, I wish to thank all those – in various quarters – who stimulated my own thinking and whose interest proved invaluable in carrying out this project.

F. Leslie Seidle
Research Director
IRPP Governance Program

1. See Kenneth Kernaghan, "Empowerment and public administration: revolutionary advance or passing fancy?", *Canadian Public Administration,* Vol. 35, no. 2 (Summer 1992), pp. 194-214 and Jerry Frug, "Administrative Democracy," *University of Toronto Law Journal,* Vol. 40 (1990), pp. 559-86.

2. See Kenneth Kernaghan, "Partnership and public administration: conceptual and practical considerations," *Canadian Public Administration,* Vol. 36, no. 1 (Spring 1993), pp. 57-76.

3. For further discussion of these types of reform and the "cultural change" approach, see Monique Jérôme-Forget, "Opening Remarks" and F. Leslie Seidle, "Rapporteur's Comments," both in this volume.

4. James Q. Wilson underlines the importance of defining a core mission for an organization, distributing authority and the control over resources to the tasks the organization is performing and judging organizations by results; see *Bureaucracy* (New York: Basic Books, Inc., 1989).

5. David Osborne and Ted Gaebler, *Reinventing Government* (Reading, Mass.: Addison-Wesley Publishing Company, 1992).

6. *Reinventing Government* includes numerous case studies of government innovation at the state and local level in the US. See also David Osborne, *Laboratories of Democracy* (Boston: Harvard Business School Press, 1990).

7. David E. Rosenbaum, "Remaking Government," *The New York Times,* September 8, 1993, pp. A1, B10.

8. In a letter to all federal civil servants, Clerk of the Privy Council Glen Shortliffe reportedly indicated that a "fundamental review" of federal policies and programs would begin in November 1993 (Hugh Winsor, "Axe to fall on another batch of civil servants," *The Globe and Mail,* September 9, 1993, p. A3A). See also John Geddes, "Taking aim at bureaucracy's bloat," *The Financial Post,* July 31, 1993, p. 5.

ACKNOWLEDGEMENTS

Financial contributions from those listed below assisted IRPP in organizing the roundtable, "Rethinking Government: Reform or Reinvention?" and in publishing this volume. This generous support is gratefully acknowledged.

The Secretary of State of Canada

Ministère de la main-d'oeuvre, de la sécurité du revenu et de la
    formation professionnelle, Gouvernement du Québec

Ville de Montréal

Gaz Métropolitain

Imasco Limited

Téléglobe Canada Inc.

École nationale d'administration publique

M O N I Q U E   J É R Ô M E - F O R G E T

OPENING REMARKS

The title of this roundtable was chosen to reflect the challenge that confronts governments and citizens at a time when the old ways of governing are being questioned in a fundamental manner. The title also presents a challenge to those who have decided to join this debate, whose comments and ideas can contribute to our search for new ways of conducting public affairs.

We have ample evidence from the past two decades or so, and not only in Canada, that internal tinkering in relation to government administration at various levels is no longer adequate. Changes such as less centralized financial controls and delayering, while valid in themselves, are only bandages. The problems and the challenges are far more fundamental. What seems to be necessary is, frankly, rethinking what we have taken for "government" up to now. I suggest this should embrace at least three perspectives.

First, we need to look at the size and structure of government. In many ways, we seem stuck in the old mindset that government should be involved in almost every area, solve almost any problem. We have seen government organization proliferate: as Gordon Osbaldeston has documented, there are over 300 organizations in the federal public sector.[1] Inevitably this has enlarged the span of control of government. But there is little reason to believe it has led to more coherent government decision making or helped government set clear priorities and carry them through.

There is also the question of the number of public servants. In an article for *Policy Options,* Leslie Seidle, using previously unpublished Statistics Canada data, indicates that if Crown corporations are excluded federal government employment in 1992 was slightly higher than at the end of the Trudeau era.[2]

We can draw a contrast with the European Community which, although not a full federation, exercises significant powers in relation to the 12 member countries. The Community has some 12,000 employees with administrative responsibilities. We have more than 400,000 federal employees serving 27 million people.

There is no doubt that stormy waters lie ahead for Canada. The state of our public finances will dictate an agenda of concerted action to reduce deficits and debt. This will take place in the midst of economic restructuring, a slow recovery, continuing high unemployment, a more open trading environment and tough international competition. These factors and others require that we take a hard look at what constitutes the essential business of government. For what remains, we need to consider other avenues.

Reviewing the essential tasks of government should lead to simpler and more coherent structures. We are told that the de Cotret study proposed that the federal government be reduced to some 15 departments. We do not know how this recommendation was reached, but it suggests the task may not be as elusive as some would think. Unfortunately, the report is still secret. The thrust of this exercise must be revived not only as part of a review of the cost of government, but also as a way of ensuring the federal government best performs what it needs to do.

In his paper, Paul Thomas suggests that in the future government organizations will have to be "anticipatory, flexible, responsive, inquisitive, innovative and adaptive." This is indeed a tall order! While Thomas wisely reminds us of the differences between private- and public-sector organizations, he nevertheless concludes that we can learn from recent research on organizational change in the private sector.

As I see it, rethinking government requires a second perspective in addition to questions of size and structure. We must address how governments work, particularly how decisions are taken and how departments and agencies are managed. In their paper for this roundtable, Bill Jenkins and Andrew Gray refer to the 1988 Ibbs Report, which led to major changes in government structure in the UK. The report concluded that:

- the civil service was too large to manage as a single organization;
- ministerial overload diverted attention from management matters;
- the freedom of middle managers was being frustrated by hierarchical controls; and
- there was little emphasis on the achievement of results.

I was struck by how pertinent these observations are to the Canadian context.

Some of these themes are also central to the very important book, *Reinventing Government,* by David Osborne and Ted Gaebler.[3] I agree with David Siegel's comment in his paper for this conference that the book was a breath of fresh air which arrived at just the right time. "Reinventing government" has indeed become a byword for examining not only how government is structured, but also how it works as an organization. There is much to the authors' recommendation that government organization should be mission-driven (that is driven by goals, not rules and regulations) as well as result-oriented (measuring performance to determine among, other things, the pay levels of employees).

Changing the "culture" of an organization as a way to improve how government works internally is one route. It has its merits, but it falls short of citizens' heightened expectations. And it is clear to me that one cannot change perception and the way civil servants think before changing their behaviour. There is ample evidence that you must first change behaviour and that changes in perception follow.

This leads me to the third perspective that deserves attention, the relation between government and citizens — in particular, how government serves Canadians. On the latter count, evidence suggests that the federal government does not do as well as it should. A 1992 Insight Canada Research survey on service to the public indicated that:

- the federal civil service received the lowest rating of eight organizations (including provincial and municipal governments);
- respondents ranked municipal governments higher than the provincial and federal governments; and
- 31 percent said service from the federal government had declined in the previous five years.[4]

While these data may be partly explained by increased cynicism toward governments generally, they should lead us to reflect. The fact that taxpayers and consumers rate government services so lowly has ramifications beyond a particular transaction. Citizens expect prompt, helpful and courteous service from both public- and private-sector organizations. If taxpayers believe they are being cheated, we should not be surprised when bureaucrat-bashing becomes part of political discourse.

Osborne and Gaebler provide numerous examples of alternative delivery mechanisms that can result in improved service to the public. They strongly argue that governments need to focus more on "steering," or developing policy, than on "rowing" — that is, actually delivering services. In addition, we have a great deal to learn from what has been happening in the United Kingdom. The Next Steps program, combined with a later initiative, the Citizen's Charter, reflects a heightened sensitivity toward service to the British public.

In rethinking how government serves the public, a range of options should be considered. Contracting out and privatization may make sense in some situations but not in others. Performance targets — very much part of the Next Steps program — are potentially useful, but some government activities are not readily quantified. Service testing and assessment should also be considered where appropriate.

While no one route will be the ideal across the board, there is a general point that is relevant to all attempts to improve service to the public. The results will almost certainly be more significant if bolstered by political will. This is also true of the other perspectives on rethinking government I've just sketched. Our political leaders need to provide a vision for reform. They need to support change, but they also must stand behind and encourage those who continue to provide services to a more diverse and more demanding public. Our political leadership, drawing on recent experience, would do well to reflect on how best to involve the public in the development of sensible public policies and regulations — an area Liora Salter addresses in her paper.

It is entirely fair to say that this roundtable is a partnership. Without the support and interest I found in various quarters, we could not have proceeded with this event. I look forward to a lively discussion and hope by the end we shall have a better idea of at least some of the remedies we might apply as we rethink the role and structure of government and the way it serves Canadians.

1. Gordon Osbaldeston, *Organizing to Govern* (Toronto: McGraw-Hill Ryerson, 1992), Vol. 1, p. 1.
2. F. Leslie Seidle, "Reshaping the Federal Government: Charting the Course," *Policy Options,* Vol. 14, no. 6 (July-August 1993), p. 28.
3. David Osborne and Ted Gaebler, *Reinventing Government* (Reading, Mass.: Addison-Wesley Publishing Company, 1992).
4. Insight Canada Research, *Perspectives Canada,* Vol. 1, no. 4 (Fall 1992).

SITUATING THE DEBATE

ON GOVERNMENT REFORM

Bonjour, educators. I say "educators" because all of us have to do some extensive re-education of our peoples, since clearly government is not going to be allowed to stay as it is.

I come from California, although I was born and raised in Cleveland. My interest in government started because I wanted to be mayor of Cleveland. In the late 1940s and 1950s that city had a dumb mayor; he wasn't corrupt, he was just dumb. And I said, "this can be done better." Yet it seemed to me that running for office had three distinct disadvantages. One is that you had to stick around in one community all the time; two, you had to get elected; and three, you didn't get paid very much. I was not terribly excited about the prospects of running for mayor, even though I thought I could perhaps bring a bit of change.

Imagine my excitement when as a freshman in college I discovered there was a position called city manager. Often city managers move around, usually by their own volition; but often they move on because the mayor has asked them to do so. Secondly, you don't have to stay in one community all the time in order to get elected because city managers are not elected. And thirdly, the city manager is often the highest paid person in the city. So I choose at age 17 to enter government service. I chose very consciously the local level, rather than the federal or state level, for the purpose of being able to influence the quality of life and serve citizens. And I thought I could do my apprenticeship at the local level and move up, which is apparently what has happened.

I come to you then as a pragmatic practitioner, and it is an honour for me to be invited by a prestigious organization such as the IRPP. I am not an academic. I do not spend my time thinking grand thoughts and developing grand theories. I spend my time trying to solve problems and meet budgets and deal with irate citizens. I have slowly learned, from a very different perspective in the cauldron of real service delivery systems, why it is we need to change government.

Our work on reinventing government started not because of some grand scheme. We started out to solve problems and accidentally we found something that was different. When David Osborne and I did our five-year survey of governments in the United States and Canada, and indeed around the world, we were able to see that a pattern was emerging; there was something different from what we had been used to seeing. We offered our book as the very beginning — rough draft efforts. We thought of ourselves as cartographers as they must have been in Italy in the 1400s, 1500s and 1600s, when, using little bits of information the explorers would bring back, they tried to put together an image of the new world. We offered our book as an image, a very rough draft image, of the new world. It is our fond hope that it will become rapidly obsolete as citizens and government officials like you become involved in writing the next chapters, the principles 12 through 20. And we are beginning to see that emerge already; we are finding that some of the things we chronicled in our book have been superseded by people actually in the arena making change.

I want to use this time to build a picture of the context in which we see change occurring. It is absolutely essential that we spend our time thinking about rethinking government. In that regard, one of my favourite philosophers is an old-time American baseball player, Satchel Paige. He was reported to have a saying, among his many sayings, that "it is not what you don't know that hurts you, it is what you think you know that just ain't so."

What I find, and why I addressed you as educators, is that people — citizens, government officials, elected people and particularly the media — carry around information about government that is wrong. As a result, the value systems upon which they have internalized their beliefs are wrong. In most cases the information was wrong when they got it, let alone wrong in the light of how society is changing today. In fact, when I tried to initiate change as city manager, I found that I had to go talk to the Rotarians and the downtown merchants and the industrialists and the ex-elected officials, and get permission for each and every initiative that we tried. I did this because we were listening to the heavy, steady drumbeat of the public saying, "we want you to change, we do not support government the way it is." In an effort not to have to make individual pleas for, and build consensus on, each and every initiative, I was interested in writing a book that would allow a much broader discussion, which would at the same time do a lot of re-educating; blow out old information, wrong belief systems and inaccurate data; and allow people to see that in fact government can be responsive, can change.

It has always amused me that in our private lives we look forward each year to the new styles of clothes, the new ties, the new cars, the new PCs or software or the new CDs. In the private sector we always look forward to new things. But in government we never do! In fact we look askance at things that are new. So part of my life has been spent trying to change the mindset of opinion shapers in the community so they in turn will not only allow us in government to change; they will demand that we change in harmony with the value system of each country, of each province, of each municipality. And so the effort to blow out a lot of old information is why I have become an educator.

It is said that 90 percent of what we know we have learned since high school. Forty-two new nations have joined the United Nations since I went to high school; 30 African nations have new names. When I was born, 52 percent of Americans smoked; now 18 percent of Americans do. We have learned about gene splicing and satellites and PCs and cellular phones and satellite uplinks and DNA. The Soviet Union is no more, and neither is Czechoslovakia or Yugoslavia; but Germany is back, which I never thought I would see in my lifetime.

How many of you have heard of AT&T? How many of you have heard of AT&T in the last two years? Think about that. We believed — probably wrongly — that AT&T was the most blue-chip, stable, well-recognized institution on earth, with the possible exception of the Catholic church. With a little help from MCI and Sprint and a few others, we have totally erased the memory of one of the most stable, blue-chip institutions on earth.

Twenty years ago, four percent of Americans pumped their own gas; today, 96 percent of Americans pump their own gas. So things do change. And when you have the perspective that things change, it is not too hard to imagine that government in fact can change through the conscious effort of people who are willing to roll up their sleeves and devote some portion of their time to that — citizens, business leaders, opinion-shapers, those who work in government at all levels. It is absolutely possible for governments to change consciously and wilfully. That is a fundamental belief of mine, and I have devoted my entire life either as an administrator or as an organizational development consultant or speaker or writer to ensuring that governments in fact can change.

I think we can agree that the very basic mission of government — in fact what we are all about — is to help citizens have a better life: a quality of life that improves commensurately with their own ability and commensurately with the ability of society to provide for that. This leads us back to governance, which is the way in which we as a society collectively make our decisions using the full resources of our society —not just governmental resources and certainly not just tax resources.

In the process of changing government, we have to pay attention to the role of the federal government, the role of the provincial governments, the role of the municipal governments and so on. In the US, we have 86,000 governments employing 19 million people, with another 600,000 elected officials who for some reason are not listed as working for government. One out of six Americans works for government. We are spending 30 percent of our nation's Gross Domestic Product on all those governments combined. That is a tremendous industry, and it is a considerable challenge to drive the forces of change. But the American public, like the world public, seems to be turning away from government.

In 1932, when Franklin Roosevelt came to power, the American public was spending 20 percent, or one-fifth of every dollar, on government services. In 1976, we reached our high-water mark of 38.4 percent, or two-fifths; Canada was then at more than 50 percent, France at more than 50 percent, Sweden at 72 percent, England at 56 percent and of course Russia at 90 percent. In the past 16 years the net buying power in the US has dropped from 38.4 percent to 30 percent; despite the Reagan Defence department buildup, our buying power has dropped by 20 percent over the past 16 years. During that same period, buying power in Canada dropped from more than 50 per cent to 34 per cent. The figure in France dropped to 41 percent during that period; Sweden went from 72 percent to 48 percent; England has gone from 56 percent to 40 percent. The figure in Russia of course has dropped to less than 70 percent from more than 90 per cent.

As we approach the end of the 20th century, it is astonishing to imagine that people are turning away from the great experiment of having government do things to provide for their quality of life. They seem to be turning away from that, whether it is in a communist nation, a Marxist nation, a socialist nation, or a capitalist nation. That is a fundamental shift that we who are in and around and paying attention to government need to consider.

People are turning away from government not only because they have been dissatisfied with how governments have delivered services, but also because they now have alternatives. David Osborne and I found that, not only was there a disenchantment with what we were doing, but in fact there were competitors out there. We in government, monopolistic as we were, did not see that coming. Let me give you a couple of examples.

In 1972, our postal service spent three years debating whether to go from an 11-cent stamp to a 14-cent stamp. In 1972, Federal Express was born and proved that people would pay US$12.75 to get something there, guaranteed overnight, while the postal service was fooling around with 11 cents to 14 cents. Today our postal service delivers 66 percent junk mail, Christmas cards and bills. Anything else you want to get to anybody else you fax, you modem, you hand carry, or you courier, you satellite uplink, you tele-conference, you telephone. It is astonishing the market share our postal service has lost over that period. They did not understand they were in a competitive market. Eight years later, they came back with express mail, trying to undercut the market at US$8.25. They still are not doing a very good job of making the service available because we have so many other choices.

The second example is that in 1970 Jackie Sorensen invented aerobics and proved that people would go to a clean, well-lit health club and pay for fitness information and nutrition information, rather than going to the old city-run or YMCA-run weight room and lift weights with those 500-pound guys who didn't smell very good. So many inter-city and city-run recreation programs closed their doors, and our staff sat there and said: "I wonder where the people are? Oh well, who cares, I get paid anyway." They did not have a sense of ownership, which is clearly one of the things that we will talk about today — how you inject ownership into a government service.

The last example is police departments. There are 3.25 million police officers in the US — 1.25 million are on the public payroll and nearly twice as many, two million, in the private sector. These private-sector officers are doing very sophisticated, anti-terrorist, anti-industrial espionage, anti-hacker, anti-satellite thievery work; and high-tech, high-pay, low-risk, often interesting overseas work. The fourth largest police department in California, a state with 33 million people, is at Bechtel. It has more police on its payroll than the city of San Jose, which has 900,000 people.

Today in the US, there is not a single business that we in government used to be in exclusively, at any level, that is not somewhere being provided by the private sector: not the enrichment of uranium, the printing of money, the collection of taxes, the running of prisons, the adjudication of justice, the prosecution of justice, the making of munitions or the conduct of overseas diplomacy. All these tasks are being done by the private sector in competition with the public sector. We in the public sector did not see that coming; we did not understand that there was in fact a competitive environment out there and that we were losing market share.

It is in this context that we need to see government: that it is in a competitive environment and is going to need to change to be competitive. And, by the way, it is also true that people in governments are doing things that heretofore the private sector used to do. There are very few things that the private sector used to do that government somewhere is not doing too. And so entrepreneurship in government is not just getting out of the business; it is in fact getting into businesses, depending on the value system of the community in which it operates.

Let me just say a final word about the context in which we find change occurring. We are finding people injecting a sense of ownership into government. Public employees are beginning to think and act like owners. Owners care about their customers; owners care about the revenue side, not just the expenditure side. We are very careful expenditure-trained people, but we are not very good at all on the revenue-raising side. One of the most exciting things we have discovered in our research is what is happening on the revenue-raising side — the non-tax, non-fee, revenue-raising side of government. Having people with a sense of ownership means that they are always focussing on dropping services and programs that have long since outlived their need. They don't do things bureaucratically; rather, they do things in a smooth, seamless way.

It has always amused me that when politicians find government revenues are dropping, the media and politicians say there are two choices: cut programs or raise taxes. It seems to me there are so many other choices. People can use assets to fund things; people can create partnerships with other people. Government can become entrepreneurial and focus on the revenue-raising side. They can focus on the internal side of government.

The conclusion of our book, above anything else, is that we in government have good people trapped in bad systems — terrible accounting systems, worse personnel systems, terrible budget systems with absolutely the wrong incentives, incentives to spend money rather than to save money, archaic outmoded communications systems or agenda processes for passing legislation, outmoded hierarchical management styles, often times male-dominated, terrible systems. Not bad people. Good people. The people we spoke to in our research said somewhere between 15 and 30 percent of the dollars that are spent by government are spent on supporting outmoded, archaic, centralized systems that add to the costliness of government and the perception of inefficiency.

One last comment. The citizen doesn't care which government delivers services. Citizens want a seamless opportunity for getting their needs taken care of. They do not care, when they dial an emergency number, whether it is an emergency physician responding or a paramedic funded by government, or whether it is a non-profit organization, or what it is. They don't care. When I turned on the water this morning in the hotel, I had no idea whether I was turning on a public water system, a private water system or if the water had been brought from a cistern or a well. I had no idea where the water came from; nor did I care.

Citizens don't care who delivers. They don't care if it is the provincial government, municipal government, federal government, a consortium of governments, or not government at all. They will pick and choose among many competing vendors for services, and they want a seamless operation. We in government have always thought of ourselves as service providers, when in fact that is not relevant to citizens any more. And so we need to spend some time rethinking what our role and mission is as we face the end of the twentieth century and look forward to a very different environment not just here in Canada or the US, but worldwide.

COPING WITH CHANGE:

HOW PUBLIC AND PRIVATE ORGANIZATIONS READ

AND RESPOND TO TURBULENT EXTERNAL

ENVIRONMENTS

P A U L   G .   T H O M A S

Coping with Change: How Public and Private Organizations Read and Respond to Turbulent External Environments

Introduction

It is a truism that the world around us is changing rapidly. Writers compete with one another to find the most vivid metaphor to describe the velocity and unpredictability of change in the external environments of most organizations. Whereas organizations once paddled on calm lakes and faced only occasional storms they now must deal, according to one writer, with "permanent white water."[1] There are no longer periods when organizations and individuals can rest and absorb the impacts of previous waves of change. Not only is change seen to be continuous, it is also said to be tumultuous in terms of the social, economic, technological and political upheavals involved. The scope and depth of the changes taking place is said to require a fundamental rethinking of the conceptual models or paradigms upon which organizations have been built in the past. Successful organizations of the future, it is often suggested, will be those which are anticipatory, flexible, responsive, inquisitive, innovative and adaptive.

In most of the popular management literature dealing with organizational change there are comforting connotations of predictability, direction, control and precision. Important features of organizational life that complicate the change process and make successful adaptation less than certain tend to be ignored or at least underestimated in the literature. This paper argues that when fundamental organizational changes are involved, the process is usually difficult, protracted, discontinuous and often conflictual. Additional constraints and complications are involved when efforts are made to change public sector organizations. However, generalizations about the difficulties of change must be approached cautiously because, contrary to the popular stereotype of a monolithic homogeneous institution, the public sector is actually a vast agglomeration of very diverse organizations. Confident and optimistic recommendations for the management of change in general terms do not take sufficient account of the differences among public organizations in terms of their environments, core tasks, formal structures of authority, leadership approaches, informal patterns of power and influence and the openness of their cultures to change.

This paper does not purport to present a grand theory of how the characteristics of an organization affect its capacity to respond to external pressures and challenges. Existing theoretical knowledge has not been refined to the point where we can identify precisely the relationships among various components of organizational life for the purpose of consciously and deliberately managing change. More modestly, I seek to identify as comprehensively as possible the variables relevant to organizational change, and to suggest links among them. However, practicing managers cannot wait for theory development to take place before they must act. This paper offers some suggestions for overcoming organizational inertia and barriers to change. It is based in part on the findings from the first stage of a research project dealing with how four organizations — three public and one private — notice, interpret and respond to changes in their external environments.

The paper is structured as follows. First, the concepts of organizational environments and of organizational change will be examined. Despite the popularity of these terms in the management literature, their meanings are far from being settled. Secondly, the significant differences between the public and private sector in terms of their external environments, internal decision-making requirements and the nature of their product or service are presented briefly to explain why change is more complicated for governments. The implications of size, complexity and diversity for the change process are also examined in this section.

Thirdly, the preliminary findings from the research study of how four organizations interact with their environments are presented. A fourth section provides some insights into how various factors are related in the process of large-scale organizational change.

The overall conclusion is that there is no one best approach to the management of change. Instead the strategy followed should be contingent on both external environmental circumstances and the internal conditions of the particular organization involved. Given the uncertainties of organizational life, creative strategic improvisation will probably be more important than formal strategic planning for most organizations.

THE KEY CONCEPTS: ENVIRONMENTS AND CHANGE

Today's managers are frequently exhorted to pay more attention to the world outside their organizations; to practice what Gareth Morgan calls management from the "outside in" as opposed to management from the "inside out."[2] For organizations to be more aware of and responsive to outside trends and developments, they will have to become more effective at performing three crucial steps: scanning the external environment to capture relevant signals, interpreting the significance of outside events for the future of the organization and taking appropriate actions within the organization to align it with anticipated environmental conditions. If these three steps are performed successfully, the result is presumed to be improved organizational performance and long-term viability.

The term "environment" is used very generally in the literature to refer to all factors beyond the boundary of the organization that have the potential to affect all or part of the organization.[3] For large multi-functional organizations, there is likely to be several rather than just one environment. Depending upon the issue or the level of the organization affected, the relevant environment will differ. Drawing a line between the organization and its environment is not always straightforward, especially in the case of public sector bodies which are open to short-term political pressures.

Despite the frequent exhortations to managers to develop a stronger external orientation, there are relatively few concrete methods identified in the literature for reading the signals from the environment.[4] Various conceptual frameworks have been developed to identify different dimensions of organizational environments, but these tend to be rather general and not easily operationalized by managers. For example, a distinction is often made between the primary or task environments of organizations and their secondary or general environments. Typically, organizations are more attentive to their task environments.

Another approach, described as PEST analysis in the strategic planning literature, divides the environment into four sections — political, economic, social and technological — for the purpose of scanning for threats and opportunities.[5] A final approach presents a descriptive analysis of environments in terms of such dichotomies as simple vs. complex, connected vs. disjointed, placid vs. turbulent, predictable vs. unpredictable, and resource munificence vs. resource scarcity.[6] Using such categories, some writers recommend that organizational strategies, structures and processes should be adapted to environmental contingencies, as well as to other contingencies. For example, Nutt and Backoff suggest that "bureaucratic strategies" are appropriate for simple and placid environments, but when turbulent, complex and disjointed environments are involved, so-called "mutualist strategies" should be followed.[7] Unfortunately, these efforts to describe different dimensions of organizational environments have not been refined to the point where we can offer coherent theories about how to match organizational designs and internal processes to anticipated environmental conditions.

The assessment of external environments is not a simple, straightforward task. The act of noticing changes in the environment is at least as much a subjective process as it is an objective process of reacting to environmental requirements.[8] It is seldom the case that external pressures build up to a point that an organization is forced to respond and the nature of the response is obvious. What people notice about the outside world and how they interpret trends is conditioned, to some not easily specified degree, by both individual and organizational factors, such as the limits of individual human cognition and the prevailing power structure.

In their review of the literature on the cognition of problem recognition, Keisler and Sproull note such tendencies as overlooking the importance of subtle, long-term trends, the inference of cause and effect when events are connected only fortuitously, and the powerful shaping force of preconceptions and stereotypes, to name but a few factors at the individual level which complicate problem recognition.[9] Power and politics operating on several levels within organizations can also present significant barriers to problem recognition and change.[10] Usually, organizational change means a gain for some people and a loss for others. As Kaufman suggests, differences of opinion about whether organizational change is necessary and what changes should be made often divide the leaders of an organization.[11]

Finally, the climate and culture of an organization play a significant role in determining whether external developments are perceived and addressed. An entrenched culture can produce a blindness to outside changes and a stifling of internal debate. Clearly these subjective dimensions complicate the analysis of environments, but it also makes that activity more important. If the environment of an organization is to a large extent subjectively defined by individuals and by group processes, there is a need to encourage debate about what are the most salient features of the environment and about the implications of these features for the future of the organization.

There are disagreements in the literature about the primacy of external and internal causes of organizational change. Some theorists have held that organizations are incapable, regardless of will, of changing rapidly enough to accommodate external changes. Kaufman notes that " ... organizations by and large are not capable of more than marginal changes, while the environment is so volatile that marginal changes are frequently insufficient to ensure organizational survival."[12] This "strong view" of environmental impacts conflicts with a large segment of the management literature which celebrates the role of bold and visionary leaders and the creative use of foresight to keep organizations from decline or failure. We should also not ignore the fact that randomness and luck can play a part in the success and failure of organizations in ways that rational planning models do not adequately recognize.

Whether organizational change can be planned, managed or simply happens depends to a significant extent on the type of external developments involved and the consequential requirements for internal adaptation. There is much talk today about so-called "frame-breaking" changes which by the breadth and depth of their impacts cause organizations to rethink completely their purposes, structures, processes and cultures.[13] Other writers differentiate between first-order and second-order change in terms of the underlying driving forces (why change occurs), the process of change (how change occurs) and the content of change (what dimensions or levels of the organization are affected). Second-order or transformative change is said to have an impact on the overall paradigm or world view of the organization including its mission, core processes and culture.[14] Given what was said earlier about the subjectivity of individual perceptions of change, there is obviously room for debate within organizations about whether particular external developments are fundamental in nature. In terms of internal changes, most are designed not to transform the organization but to fine-tune it to deal with perceived problems. Organizations are never completely at rest. There is always motion within them, but when the changes are incremental and resources are readily available there is less conflict and, on the surface at least, there is the appearance of stability. Although incremental changes clearly out number major transformative changes, it is an open question which type of change contributes more overall to organizational momentum and success.

Some writers go so far as to question whether organizations can recognize the need for change and then execute the change process successfully. They suggest that the most significant features of the future environments of organizations are unknown and therefore the idea of designed change is untenable.[15] Others suggest, somewhat less pessimistically, that organizations are severely constrained in their capacities to change. Most of the time, various forces of inertia are said to uphold the organizational *status quo*: financial and psychological investments in existing strategies and polices; a desire not to disrupt the equilibrium of power and influence, and the hold that the prevailing cultural paradigm of the organization has on the thinking of its members. These perspectives represent the structural inertia view of organizations. More optimistically, other commentators insist that organizations do have the capacity to adapt to their environments and they point to the crucial role played by visionary, bold and astute leaders in achieving organizational innovation. This is the strategic choice school of thinking.

Another perspective suggests that organizations may not need to respond to external change at all or may only need to respond in symbolic ways. For example, Meyer and Scott suggest that for public organizations (they focused mainly on schools) there is a "logic of confidence" which allows organizations to remain substantively unchanged provided they are seen as embodying the right kinds of activities regardless of outcome.[16] In a related piece of writing, Meyer and Zucker focus on what they call "the permanently failing organization."[17] They argue that organizations are places in which multiple competing interests are at play. The achievement of organizational goals may be a low priority compared to the satisfaction of these interests. The insistence that organizations must respond to their environments is misleading because many organizations act deliberately to resist such a response. Lack of response, according to Meyer and Zucker, is not a failure by the organization, but a fundamental characteristic of it. In this view, persistence of the organization is not always related to its success in serving its official goals.

Only a selective review of the mammoth literature on organizational change has been presented above. An effort has been made to clarify some of the ambiguity surrounding the terms "environment" and "change" as these apply to organizations. Leaders of organizations have been told to pay more attention to the outside world, but the techniques for discovering and analyzing external forces are not well developed. What is noticed in the environment and how developments are interpreted are not purely objective processes; they are affected by both individual and organizational factors. Subjective perceptions of change, taking place both externally and internally, will vary among people within the same organizations. Uncertainty about the direction and implications of change, internal competition for power and resources, resistance to change within the organizational culture, and perhaps even an absence of external pressures to adapt, have all been identified as factors which complicate the change process. Most organizations and the people in them cherish stability. Regardless of the type of organization involved, there are clear limitations to managerial action in making change happen. The popular stereotype of the visionary and bold leader who transforms the organization to meet what, to others, are dimly perceived future challenges is inspirational but there are a number of reasons to doubt that it fits the realities of most organizations.

CHANGE IN THE PUBLIC SECTOR: THE COMPLICATIONS OF DIVERSITY AND SIZE

Most of the literature on organizational change is based on the study of private firms, although research on change in the public sector is growing. Controversy exists over whether the public and the private sector represent completely different kinds of management challenges.[18]

There is a lengthy and distinguished body of literature which suggests that the commonalities among organizations should be emphasized, not the relatively unimportant distinction of whether they are public or private, profit or not-for-profit. This is the generic tradition in organizational theory. It suggests that tasks, technologies, size and the type of environments involved are more important determinants of performance than whether organizations are created, owned and funded by governments. It is noted, for example, that a government-owned hospital resembles a private hospital far more than it resembles a government department. Organizations performing the same or similar tasks will likely use the same technologies, develop similar structural arrangements and face the same challenges in terms of adaptation to the environment. According to the generic view point, good management approaches and practices will work well regardless of whether they are applied in the private or the public sector.

The opposite side in the controversy is summed up neatly in Wallace Sayre's oft-quoted aphorism that the public and the private sectors are "fundamentally alike in all unimportant respects."[19] Supporters of this view point suggest that various features of the public sector make the tasks of leadership and management more challenging than in the private sector. These features include: the pervasive influence of politics, a wider range of values and interests to be reconciled, the absence of a well-defined and universally accepted measure of success, the requirements of democratic accountability which lead to the adoption of numerous, centralized rules and procedures, and the frequency of change in political leadership and policy direction. Under these conditions, it is suggested, management approaches and techniques borrowed from the private sector will fail or work badly. The long history of transfers of private management practices to the public sector is said to have produced a singularly unspectacular record of limited success, some colossal failures and in general mediocre results.

Organizational theory and available research evidence suggest that a balanced view of this controversy is the most appropriate. First, the dividing line between public and private is blurred. Despite deregulation efforts, all private firms are still affected to a significant extent by laws and regulations, although they are not enveloped in legal restrictions to the same degree as public bodies. Many more organizations today are hybrid enterprises that belong strictly to neither the public nor the private sector, as for example with former crown corporations that have been partially privatized or private firms which are the chosen policy instruments of governments for purposes like energy development or defense procurement. In other words, the degree of "publicness" of an organization depends, not just on government auspices, ownership and funding, but also on the extent to which it is subject to government influence. Second, many decisions in public organizations are not affected by politics and institutional constraints; there is clearly scope at some levels in the bureaucracy to apply modern management approaches.

The available research evidence supports the contention of the generic school that the core task of an organization is the single most important determinant of its environment, technology, structure and management approaches, regardless of whether it is situated in the public or the private sector. Oversimplified and sharp distinctions between the two sectors should therefore be avoided. However, it is crucial to recognize that the tasks assigned to government organizations are often unique, having no counterpart in the private sector. This is the fundamental differentiating characteristic of public organizations: they are formally endowed with a public policy purpose. Most of the tasks performed by government organizations are ones that private firms would not contemplate or even may have abandoned. An underlying reason for the generally poor reputation of public organizations as effective performers is the distinctive and challenging nature of the assignments they are given. For example, it is very difficult to operate a public broadcasting network which is Canadian in character while living alongside the most powerful communications networks in the world. When evaluating the capacity of public organizations to notice external developments and to respond effectively, there must be adequate recognition of the unique tasks they are often asked to perform.

Even after a decade of efforts to scale back the size of the public sector, it still represents a vast, sprawling and diverse undertaking that relies upon a wide range of different policy instruments to achieve what are often nebulous, shifting and conflicting goals. The organizational variety, size and complexity of government operations mean that public managers face more complicated environments, a weaker sense of strategic direction and far more elaborate requirements for coordinating activities than their private sector counterparts.

Common sense and personal experience lead one to suspect that large organizations are different from small organizations. Large organizations are widely assumed to be more bureaucratic and resistant to change, to contain more administrative layers, to be less responsive to their clients and to provide less satisfaction to their employees. However, the evidence on the impact of size is inconclusive.[20] Rarely, if ever, do we find that one variable like size explains everything about an organization. First, there is controversy about how to measure size. What do we mean when we talk about "big" and "small" organizations? The most popular measurement is the number of employees, but budgets, number of clients served and the scope of their impact represent other possible measures of organizational size.

Often the comparison is made between large public bureaucracies and supertankers moving at full speed, in terms of the difficulty and time involved with the achievement of any significant change in direction. All large organizations are supposedly prone to rigidity, but public sector bodies are seen as particularly inflexible. However, the relationship between size and adaptiveness is anything but straightforward.[21] If size entails bureaucratization and insulation, then large organizations will be harder to change than smaller organizations. On the other hand, if size is related to the possession of slack resources and decentralized structures, then larger organizations can be more flexible than smaller organizations. Recent steps by governments to use decentralization to foster innovation have been made more difficult by the prevailing conditions of budgetary restraint.

Findings on the impact of size on the formality, centralization and complexity of organizational structures are also inconsistent. Some researchers assert that increased size is correlated with increased specialization, increased spatial dispersion, an increased number of hierarchical layers and an enlarged administrative component.[22] In comparison to private firms, governments usually make greater use of rules regarding personnel, budgeting, purchasing and accounting matters. However, large size does not correlate automatically with greater internal complexity and reliance upon bureaucratic red tape. Other factors, such as information technology, can be used to overcome somewhat the limits of hierarchy and physical separation, and the rule orientation of public bureaucracies can be reduced.

In addition to rigidity and internal structural complexity, large size is suspected of contributing to employee dissatisfaction and poor motivation. Large organizations are seen as impersonal; people do not see how their activities relate to organizational goals and often they feel that their ideas are "lost in the pipeline" to the top of the organization. On the other hand, larger organizations provide some people with greater status and power, more opportunities for career advancement and greater scope for decentralization to autonomous units. The latter benefit of size has been harder to realize in government where, in the pursuit of "error-free" administration, central agencies have retained strict controls over departmental procedures, and within departments senior managers have been reluctant to delegate meaningful decision-making authority to personnel at the field level.

Morale problems among managers within governments seem very serious at this time. The malaise is especially pronounced among middle managers who feel underutilized and underappreciated. They are also concerned about job security as a result of downsizing, consolidation and administrative streamlining. Two surveys conducted by Zussman and Jabes in the late 1980s documented the frustration and alienation among managers within the federal public service.[23] The problem may be less pronounced within provincial bureaucracies whose scope and scale of operations remain small compared to official Ottawa. We lack empirical surveys equivalent to the federal studies, but based upon interviews with federal and provincial officials conducted several years ago, Graham White concluded that provincial bureaucracies were generally less paper-oriented and more people-oriented than the federal bureaucracy.[24] More specifically, he reported the following perceived differences at the provincial level: there was closer contact between politicians and officials, the translation of political priorities into policy and administrative actions was easier, less use was made of formal coordination mechanisms because there was greater reliance upon informal communication among senior officials, central agencies were less aggressive and intrusive in departmental operations, deputy ministers had greater familiarity with actual program operations and junior, less-experienced public servants were granted more responsibility. There is an important reminder here that provincial bureaucracies are not just scaled-down versions of their Ottawa counterparts and therefore do not necessarily face an identical set of problems.

During the past decade public services at both levels of government have experienced budgetary restraint, declining work forces and the rationalization of their activities through the elimination or reduction of programs, the disappearance or merger of organizations and the use of privatization and contracting out to achieve public policy goals. It has been suggested that organizational downsizing will be different during periods of abrupt and discontinuous change (reorientation periods) than during periods of incremental change and adaptation (convergent periods).[25] Down sizing during reorientation periods will involve changing the missions, strategies and systems of organizations, will entail radical rather than modest design changes and will require the development of a stronger external orientation to cope successfully with change. The current period can only be described as one of reorientation. Not only have several decades of public sector expansion come to halt, but a fundamental re-examination of the role of governments is taking place. Public sector organizations are at the centre of the swirl of controversy over the future role of governments and therefore the change process is both more difficult and threatening to the people directly affected. On the other hand, as the literature on organizations suggests, it often takes the perception of a crisis to "unfreeze" the situation so real change can occur.

Not all parts of the public sector are equally and similarly affected by the forces of external change. Several broad types of organizations with widely varying functions make up the modern public service. The traditional line department still represents the main part of the public sector, but departments vary considerably in their function, size, structure and organizational cultures. Some departments have enormous policy and political significance whereas others are mainly administrative in their function. Outside the departmental framework are the so-called crown agencies, represented mainly by crown corporations and regulatory agencies. These bodies are supposedly removed from continuous ministerial involvement and central agency controls in order to enable them to operate more efficiently and flexibly. Some simplification of the crown agency domain has occurred through the privatization and deregulation efforts of governments over the past decade, but there remains a bewildering array of semi-independent bodies responsible for policy formulation and implementation in a wide variety of policy fields at both the federal and provincial levels.

Central agencies represent a third type of organization. Their purpose is to achieve some measure of common policy direction across the otherwise loose confederacy of departments and agencies and to ensure that common administrative standards are upheld. A transformation in the role of central agencies seems to be taking place that involves a move away from the micro-management of departments towards the promotion of a shared public service culture built around values like effectiveness, innovation, quality service and the empowerment of employees. A fourth category of organizations are the various advisory bodies, like task forces and royal commissions. Finally, there are a variety of organizations that report directly to Parliament, such as the Auditor General and the Official Languages Commissioner. These parliamentary bodies were created to provide scrutiny of the regular bureaucracy, and over the years they have become more numerous and prominent. In summary, despite all the rhetoric (and to a lesser extent action) about the need to streamline governments, the bureaucratic landscape remains very cluttered. The introduction of fundamental changes into such an expansive, diversified and interconnected system is far more complicated than managing change for an individual firm.

The crowded and intersecting world of the public sector means that a major preoccupation for managers of individual organizations are the actions and reactions of other institutions and actions. For public managers the establishment of boundary spanning networks and the ongoing conduct of external relations is a critical requirement for organizational effectiveness. As part of the wider political system, all public organizations are exposed, to a greater or lesser extent, to a secondary environment that includes social, economic, technological and political forces. Many of these pressures are short-term in nature and create great uncertainty in terms of longer-range planning. Public organizations have their own distinctive internal cultures that reflect their tasks and histories, but they are also immersed in the wider administrative culture of government and the general political culture of the society at large. Developments at all three levels of culture affect the requirements for and capacity to change on the part of different public bodies. Because each organization must deal with a somewhat distinct task or primary environment, the requirements for change will vary.

In summary, the factors relevant to the process of organizational change in the public sector are numerous, and the available literature lacks precision in explaining the links among them. Differences in the tasks, size and structures of public organizations condition the external requirements for change and the capacity of organizations to respond. In general, public sector organizations must deal with environments that are more complicated, interconnected and turbulent than those of most private firms. Research on the change process within the public sector is underdeveloped at this point. Our knowledge has not been refined to the point where we can match with complete confidence the strategies, structures, actions and cultures of public organizations to some forecast of future environmental conditions. The organizational diversity of the public sector also means that there is no one right way to manage change. The successful management of change cannot be reduced to a list of steps. Essential for success in the crucial processes of reading, interpreting and responding to changing environments is an intimate knowledge of the particular organization — its history, present context, policies, structures, internal climate and culture and its relationships with other organizations. As the research reported in the next section suggests, reflective practitioners often possess more knowledge of the real requirements for successful change than the celebrity authors of the management best-sellers give them credit for, and often they underestimate their own capacities to cope with change.

THE RESEARCH PROJECT

In collaboration with Professor Benjamin Levin, the author undertook during 1991-92 a research project dealing with how four organizations respond to changes in their external environments. Three of the organizations were in the public sector and the fourth was in the private sector. The organizations varied in their tasks, size and organizational complexity; this was partly the basis for their selection. Their willingness to open their internal dynamics to study was the other main basis on which the four organizations were chosen.

- Agriculture Canada is a large federal department with about 12,000 staff, a direct budget of about $2 billion (1991-92) and spending authority over another $25 billion through various crown agencies. With 70 percent of its employees working outside the national capital, Agriculture Canada is one of the more decentralized federal departments. The department is organized in terms of three broad areas of programming: the Agri-Food programs, the Management and Administration program, and the Grains and Oilseeds Program. The research focussed mainly on the latter program. During the time the research was conducted the department was absorbing the impacts of a federal-provincial policy review, the issuance of a discussion paper (*Growing Together*) intended to set policy directions for the future, the adoption of a new mission statement and several reorganizations.

■ The Health Sciences Centre in Winnipeg is the cornerstone of health care service and education in the province of Manitoba. It is the result of an earlier merger of four separate institutions and occupies nine city blocks in the "core area" of the city, an area characterized by low incomes and living standards, ethnic and racial diversity, and a high incidence of poor health and violence. The hospital employs about 5,000 staff, there are approximately 800 physicians who work on a fee-for-service basis, and the annual budget is $275 million (1991-92), almost all (95 percent) of which comes in the form of provincial grants. HSC operates more than 200 clinical programs spread across more than 40 medical sectors. During the research period the HSC was recovering from a month-long, province-wide nurses' strike, was engaged in a budget cutback exercise, was part of a process conducted by the Urban Hospital Council to rationalize hospital services in the city and was negotiating with provincial authorities to conclude a massive physical redevelopment plan.

■ The Seven Oaks School Division is a suburban school division in Winnipeg that provides primary and secondary education to 8,000 students in 22 schools. The population served is very mixed, ethnically and economically. The division has 800 staff and an annual budget of approximately $50 million. The division faced budgetary restraint, a provincially sponsored review of the high school curriculum and internally initiated discussions involving school board members, the superintendent, staff, parents and students on the broad philosophical issue of education versus training.

■ Investors Group is a financial services company with headquarters in Winnipeg. It has approximately 2,500 staff and sales agents, does approximately $2 billion in business annually and manages approximately $14 billion in assets. The company has been growing very rapidly, even during the recession of the early nineties. It had been led by the same CEO since the late 1970s, but he was about to retire when the study began. The major challenge faced by the company was the emergence of the banks in the financial services field and the need to be aware of a changing regulatory climate.

These are thumbnail sketches of the four organizations with whom we worked. Our intention was to involve another private sector firm in the study and extend the research over several years, but unfortunately our funding ran out. We recognize the difficulty of fully understanding the context and internal dynamics of any organization based upon the relatively brief period (about a year and a half) spent on the study. We developed the study as a set of simultaneous cases, emphasizing the particularities of each organization but also looking for some similarities. The use of only four cases obviously makes generalizations hazardous, and we hope to extend the study in the future.

We have described our research approach as partnership research. Rather than simply requesting permission to collect data, we sought to involve the four organizations in the definition of the research and in the review of the findings. The result was a hybrid approach that was part social science inquiry and part management consultation. Our methods included the review of major documents (strategic plans, budgets, board minutes, etc.), interviews and limited participant observation in organizational events. Nearly 60 interviews were conducted with senior officials in the four organizations selected on the basis of their positions within the organization. The interviews were basically open-ended. While common questions were used in all interviews, in light of the exploratory nature of the research it was decided to follow up potentially interesting avenues of discussion raised by individual respondents. At the conclusion of the first phase of the study we presented interim reports to our partners for review, and these discussions were used to identify directions for the second stage of the research. We believe strongly that this collaborative approach to research on organizational change has the potential to produce both valuable theoretical and practical knowledge, but we also discovered that the institutional norms and practices to support it are not well developed in either the scholarly community or within organizations.

Two broad sets of research questions guided our enquiries into organizational adaptation: 1) How have managers and organizations noticed events, and/or developments of trends within their external environment that will have an impact on their performance; and 2) what is the link, if any, between the prevailing interpretation(s) of the environment and the agenda(s) of the organizations? Only some of the main conclusions of the study can be presented in here.

Overall, our findings suggest that the processes required for organizations to notice, interpret and respond to their environments are less straightforward, systematic and objective than most management texts imply. In each of the organizations respondents were asked to identify in an open-ended fashion what they saw as the main external challenges facing the organization. Table 1 lists the frequency of mention for various categories of issues. The table reveals a relatively strong consensus within all four organizations about what were the main external issues, but it must be remembered that interviews were conducted only with senior managers. Further down in the organization there were probably different views of the outside world. Also, the four organizations had all recently been involved in strategic planning exercises or policy reviews, so it may be that our respondents had become good at what a manager at Agriculture Canada called "spouting the party line."

While there was widespread agreement on the most important external issues facing each of the four organizations, there was far less agreement on the implications of those issues for the particular organizations involved. Perhaps not surprisingly, our respondents were somewhat reluctant to share with curious social scientists the conflicting interpretations about how the organizations must change to deal with environmental uncertainty. Some respondents had thought more deeply about and could articulate more completely than their colleagues views on how the organization should interact with the environment. These people seemed to be opinion leaders in terms of shaping the organization's outlook on the changing world.

Respondents in all four organizations believed that they now faced more turbulent and unpredictable environments than during previous periods. The response of a senior official at Agriculture Canada was typical: "The department faces a turbulent environment. In the short term, the central issue is how western farmers will survive the next five years. In the longer term, there are so many changes taking place in the world that we have to ask what agriculture will be 15 years from now." In most cases such perceptions were highly subjective since only in the financial services company had any analytical work been done on the pace of

Table 1

External Issues Identified by Respondents in the Four Organizations

<u>*School district*</u> (N=9)	<u>*Hospital*</u> (N=11)
financial pressure - 9	financial pressures - 11
changing population/clientele - 7	changing technology - 8
impact of education research - 5	scope of responsibilities - 6
impact of pressure groups - 4	relationships with other hospitals - 6
influence of the media - 3	relationships with government - 6
Others - professional development, arbi-	shifting patient demands - 5
trary government decisions, information	changing patient demographics - 4
technology, private schools, Charter of	personnel issues - 4
Rights, transportation	*Others - physical plant, labour negotia-*
	tions, changes in professional roles
<u>*Financial services company*</u> (N=8)	<u>*Agriculture Canada*</u> (N=11)
changes in client demographics	globalization and competition - 11
and needs - 8	financial restraint - 9
increased competition - 8	impact of politics - 7
changes in sales force - 6	changes in service delivery - 7
government policies - 4	changing technology - 6
expansion of French immersion - 2	Ministers' character - 5
changes in labour markets - 2	structural problems of industry - 5
changes in technology - 4	pressures from industry - 7
Others - changing values, national	agriculture as a way of life - 4
unity, overall economic conditions	food safety - 3
	envrionmental protection - 3
	Others - historical influences, federal
	government reforms national unity,
	changes in food consumption, rural-
	urban issues, multiculturalism

NOTE: These categorizations are abstracted from the interviews; respondents sometimes included quite diverse ideas which were grouped together for analytic purposes.

change. Along with a sense of accelerated change, there was doubt on the part of some respondents about whether the environment was amenable to understanding and response. "When change is continuous on almost a daily basis," stated one hospital official, "it is difficult to build a stable organizational culture."

As the list of issues reveals, drawing a boundary line between the organization and its environment was artificial for many of our respondents, especially in the public sector organizations, because officials were involved almost daily in the management of external issues. Likewise, most of our managers had not thought about the outer parameters of their organizational environments. The dichotomies used in the theoretical literature to describe different organizational environments — complex vs. simple, placid vs. turbulent, munificence vs. scarcity, etc. — were not part of the thinking of our managers. Instead of broad theoretical categories, they understood the environment in a more direct and intuitive fashion in terms of particular issues and events. These details were the conceptual handles used to gain a grasp on a universe they saw as enormously complicated and increasingly threatening. Resource acquisition was a major preoccupation for the three public organizations, especially for the hospital.

Most strategic planning texts recommend that organizations periodically scan their environments to discover threats and opportunities using such techniques as brainstorming sessions, Delphi exercises, indicators research, focus groups and surveys.[26] All four of the organizations in the study had undertaken planning exercises, but little use was made of formal analytical tools or management techniques. The environmental scanning step in such planning exercises was seen as useful, not so much in terms of discovering previously unseen dimensions of the environment, but rather in terms of making explicit an image of the organization and its environment that was already present in the minds of executives. A vice-president of planning at Investors, the organization with the most focussed intelligence gathering system of the four, observed that: "People always think that strategy ... is the result of highly knowledgeable people with vast databases of information that they have skilfully interpreted, but a lot of it is just plain seat of the pants." Other respondents talked about their awareness of the environment emerging from many sources through a process that resembled "osmosis." In all four organizations there were informal and uncoordinated processes of interaction and communication taking place continuously. Managers attended meetings, they read and circulated articles, they attended outside conferences and they maintained networks of contacts with numerous people in their fields. Although difficult to document, these submerged processes of discovery and learning seemed to be very important to the emergence of a shared definition of the environment, including a climate of ideas about how the organization might be required to change.

All four organizations had taken steps to improve both external and internal communication patterns to acquire better intelligence about the changing environment and to mobilize support for the internal changes being contemplated. A veteran of 18 years service in Agriculture Canada credited the deputy minister with a recent emphasis on consultation and responsiveness to outside groups: "Networking is now considered a very valuable tool ... Sharing ideas, getting information sending information; this is important in both noticing change and in making it happen." Similarly at the school division, the superintendent had orchestrated an ongoing dialogue among trustees, administrators, teachers, students and parents about curriculum changes designed to balance the acquisition of knowledge and skills with the development of appropriate value systems among students.

In the case of large multi-functional organizations such as Agriculture Canada or the HSC, there is both a general environment and multiple, specialized environments. Also, there are numerous points of intersection of the organization with its environments. Not surprisingly, different people, having different, often specialized, backgrounds and working in different parts and levels of the organization, will have different views on what the main external issues are. The Vice-President of Finance at the HSC was naturally preoccupied with budget cutbacks, the Vice-President of Human Resources with the state of collective bargaining and the Vice-President of Medicine with the future of various clinical programs. While such observations seem trite, they have important implications for the capacity of complex organizations to change in a coherent manner. It is too deterministic to say that what people see in the external world depends entirely on where they sit in the organization, but the combination of professional background and occupational role does affect what people notice. For example, nurses in management positions at the hospital saw both the external world and internal decision-making processes differently from physicians also serving in management roles. And similarly, the 3,500 research scientists employed by Agriculture Canada are probably little affected by the world trade and currency trends that preoccupy senior officials.

The noticing of outside changes is conditioned not only by the formal structure and internal decision-making processes, but also by the culture of the organization. Our study did not seek to document the internal cultures of the four organizations. However, the available literature suggests that the assumptions, beliefs, values and ideas held by individuals concerning an organization's purpose provide an important basis for attributing meaning to outside events. Our interviews suggested the existence of separate but overlapping and intersecting cultures within the three public sector organizations. For example, some parts of Agriculture Canada focused on the need for greater reliance upon market forces, while others were principally concerned with maintaining supply management arrangements. In contrast, the financial services company seemed to have a more unified corporate culture.

Most of the mammoth literature on organizational cultures stresses the importance of leadership in transforming cultures. Efforts at cultural change were under way in each of the organizations. An activist minister and deputy minister were embarked on a process to transform an entrenched policy culture that had dominated thinking in Agriculture Canada for decades. The process was slow, however, and the deputy minister was reported as becoming impatient. One official explained: "The issues are too sensitive to articulate a clear vision of the of the future. Up to this point (early in 1992), the change process has consisted of a search for a vision." In contrast, the profitability of Investors Group was widely attributed to a focussed strategy based upon the vision of a CEO who foresaw the new contours of the marketplace and changed the products and culture of the organization accordingly.

At times, leadership can be a crucial factor in the achievement of organizational innovation, and not all of the individuals who shape organizational thinking are in senior positions. Too heroic a view of the role of leaders in shaping cultures should be avoided, however, especially in the case of public organizations that are immersed in a system-wide administrative and political culture that individual leaders do not control. As is discussed at greater length in the conclusion, cultural change is not a magic elixir, and no one culture fits all organizational situations.

The relationships among the environment, the culture and successful performance of an organization defy simple prescription.

The second dimension of the study involved the links between the perceptions of the external world and the internal decision-making agendas of the four organizations. Based upon the data gathered to date, we can make only brief comments on this aspect of organizational change. The majority of respondents in each of the four organizations felt that longer-term fundamental issues of organizational change tended to get crowded off the organization's agenda by immediate matters of a short-term nature. This is a perennial complaint in all types of organizations. However, the review of the internal documents for the four organizations suggested the interview responses involved more than people spouting the conventional wisdom. We found that urgent operational matters tended to dominate decision-making agendas. It may be that we arrived in the organizations just when they were experiencing particularly difficult times, so the emphasis on "fighting fires" may have been particularly pronounced. For example, the hospital's strategic planning process had just been interrupted by another round of budget reductions, a province-wide nurses' strike and a series of bed closures negotiated through the Urban Hospital Council. Similarly at Agriculture Canada a carefully designed process for policy and organizational change was constantly being delayed by crises over prairie farm incomes, GATT negotiations and debates over the future of the supply management system. Our findings confirm the evidence of other studies that strategy development in most organizations tends to be episodic, intermittent and events-based.

Several of our respondents recognized that the distinction between fundamental long-term and operational short-term issues was not an absolute one. By resolving pressing issues the organization was also, in effect, often setting future directions for the organization. Most respondents were very mindful of threats to the future stability and success of the organization, but few identified the opportunities associated with change. An insightful vice-president in the hospital was atypical therefore in observing that a crisis could be seen as an opportunity to achieve organizational changes that could not be accomplished due to internal resistance during so-called normal times. This observation corresponds to the finding in the literature that significant reorientations in the direction of an organization usually only occur after two events: a decline in the performance of the organization and a change in the leadership.

Neither the hospital nor the school division had adopted formal strategic plans, which does not mean they lacked a strategy or general sense of direction. Part of the implicit strategies they were following consisted of the identification of the critical events and problems to which they felt obliged to respond. Agriculture Canada prepared strategy documents that were both broad and narrow in their focus. Investors Group had the most refined planning documents, although the executives were quick to acknowledge that improvisation was still an important part of organizational change. The absence of explicit plans and the continuous updating of those that existed in the public sector organizations meant that the dividing line between strategic planning and management control was often indistinct. Because the public organizations served a wider range of stakeholders, some with opposing positions and demands, they could not adopt as explicit and precise a strategy as that of the financial services company.

As mentioned earlier, there was some reluctance among our respondents to talk about the role that power and conflict played in the process of organizational change. This may have reflected concern about possible damage caused by the revelation of internal disagreements; it may also have reflected the prevalent cultural norm that power is not a topic for general discussion since it is seen to involve the manipulation of people.[27] There is no doubt that our respondents recognized that the use of power was necessary to make things happen within organizations. Both the formal and informal structure of power within an organization will affect which dimensions of the environment receive attention, how outside events are interpreted and whether internal resistance to change can be overcome. None of the three public organizations were to anywhere near the same extent as the private firm, hierarchical organizations that were managed and led on a top down basis. As professional bureaucracies, they were organized more on the basis of specialized knowledge, and individual managers obtained significant autonomy based on their professional expertise. This pattern was most evident in the case of the hospital. The board of directors and the senior administrators could not make strategic changes, such as modifying the range of clinical programs, without the active support of the physicians. Vague and loosely connected strategies in public organizations reflect both the complexity of the environments they face and the complications involved with the achievement of internal coordination.

Further research will be required to document the overall approach to change being followed in the four organizations. However, our preliminary impression is that the leaders in our three public organizations were practicing what Robert Behn has labelled "management by groping along" (MBGA).[28] According to Behn, successful managers "grope along" rather than grope around. They establish a general direction for the organization, but they do not employ a detailed strategy. Instead MBGA involves a sequential process of experimentation and adaptation in pursuit of a goal. Small organizational changes and accomplishments are used to facilitate learning, to foster confidence and to build support for change. From groping along, leaders learn a variety of managerial lessons and develop a repertoire of behaviours that can be applied to new situations. More successful leaders will be individuals who are more reflective, develop more diverse repertoires and became more skilled at recognizing mistaken directions earlier rather than later. Uncertainty about environmental trends, the wider range of stakeholders to be accommodated and the challenges of internal coordination, all seemed to encourage adoption of a strategy of groping along as a complement to formal strategic planning which was also taking place. Of the three public organizations, the hospital faced the greatest challenges in the management of change because of both its highly dynamic environment and its rigid internal power structure.

CONCLUSION

Despite all that is written about organizational change we know less about the subject than is commonly assumed in the management literature. Managers are urged to become masters of change. Based upon a handful of instances of apparently successful changes, models for the strategic management of change are proposed as generalizable to all organizations. There is a recipe-book type of quality to this advice. And, increasingly a standardized formula is being recommended: development of an external orientation, incorporating foresight into decision making, decentralization and delayering, the removal of bureaucratic rules, reliance upon a strong, shared culture to achieve unity of purpose, the development of the competencies of individual employees and their empowerment, and the encouragement of ongoing organizational learning.

The apparent widespread agreement on what is required for organizational change is misleading. It ignores the controversies that arise in the research on change. Moreover, this new orthodoxy represents the danger that we will lapse, not for the first time in the history of organizational theory, into thinking there is one best way to improve organizations. The new approaches have a seductive appeal for beleaguered public sector managers who are constantly being told that coping with change is the difference between organizational success and failure. An approach, like that found in this paper, which emphasizes the particularistic, complicated and problematic character of the change process, has difficulty competing with the apparent certainty and precision of the best-sellers containing checklists for creative managers. We should strive to avoid, however, another case of panacea syndrome in which simplistic models for managerial reform are launched with great fanfare only to be followed in a few years by considerable disillusionment.

This paper has suggested that ambiguity still surrounds the concept of the environments of organizations and the different types of change that take place in various external environments. The technology of external assessment is not well developed. The capacity of organizations to capture close and distant signals from their environments and to forecast future conditions is uncertain. Studies indicate that there are distinct limits on the capacity of both individuals and organizations to interpret complex environments. Whether external or internal factors are the primary driving forces of change remains open to debate. Adaptation to changing environmental requirements is affected by internal factors like size, structure, processes, leadership and culture. Concepts like strategic planning and the strategic management of change have comforting, but misleading, connotations of certainty, direction, control and precision. They do not fit with the reality that significant organizational change tends to be disorderly, disjointed and problematic. There is no magic recipe for success. Instead managers must reflect constantly on their own organizational situations and see it as the most important source for learning.

Even though public and private organizations are not completely dissimilar there are dangers with applying in the public sector models and steps to guide change based upon the experience of private firms. In terms of their distinctive tasks, environments, internal decision-making structures, cultures and exposure to outside influences, most public organizations represent a greater challenge in terms of the management of change than private sector organizations. We should also avoid the danger of ignoring the differences among public sector bodies. The relationships among environments, tasks, size, structure and culture are not easily specified. Organizations and their environmental contexts can differ widely. Whether change occurs and how it occurs will be contingent upon a wide variety of circumstances.

Structural and process innovation were once seen to be the principal basis for successful organizational change. Despite a more realistic appreciation today about the limits of structural reform as the basis for attitudinal and behavioural change, we have not completely abandoned our faith in redesigning organizations to achieve greater effectiveness. Today, public organizations are urged to adopt flexible structures based upon decentralization, empowerment and the development of new procedures for the integration of perspectives and the promotion of a shared sense of direction. Writing in 1988, Peter Drucker suggested that the organization of the future will depend on knowledge specialists, will not allow for hierarchy, and will more resemble a hospital or a university than the industrial firm which has been the model for most of the 20th century.[29] On the face of it, devolution of authority and widespread participation in decision-making should lead to more people detecting changes that take place in the environment, and an emphasis on inquiry, communication and debate should foster learning. As a general approach, this sounds very plausible.

However, not all organizations resemble universities and hospitals. Furthermore, the experience of those organizations suggests that when everyone gets into the act there is often difficulty in getting any real action. In the absence of a shared vision and values such institutions are usually characterized by a lack of coherence in decision-making and only the vaguest of premises about future direction to serve as the basis for a strategy. Furthermore, while such institutions are quite successful at promoting individual learning, they are far less successful at achieving organization-wide learning. Finally, philosophies of decentralization must recognize the constitutional requirements of ministerial responsibility and the dynamics of cabinet-parliamentary government. Taken to an extreme, the advice to public sector managers to develop their own strategies and to decentralize authority could undermine ministerial responsibility. And ministers will not for long pay the price of a loss to their political reputations when the mistakes or problems caused by more entrepreneurial bureaucrats become the focal point for opposition attacks.

The problem is illustrated by the creation of Special Operating Agencies (SOAs) throughout the federal government (following the April 1993 budget, there were 16, one on a trial basis). SOAs are meant to provide a platform for organizational change in terms of developing a stronger customer focus, reducing procedural controls and reinforcing accountability in terms of the achievement of results. It is probably premature to draw definitive conclusions about the Canadian experience with SOAs. However, New Zealand and the United Kingdom have more experience with what they call executive agencies, and the available evidence suggests that they have not entirely fulfilled their promise in terms of more responsive, effective, efficient service delivery and that the issues of democratic accountability have not been fully resolved.[30] There are other interesting developments and literature on the use of parallel learning structures within bureaucratic organizations to promote inquiry, learning and change. Bushe and Shoni describe five cases in which semi-permanent structures were added to existing organizations to solve organization-wide problems, to improve union-management relations, to add adaptive capacity, to redesign the organization on a socio-technical basis and to implement system-wide transformations.[31]

Culture has replaced structure as the most popular variable in the organizational change process. Change the culture, the message goes, and the majority of organizational problems will be solved. Despite a growing empirical research base that testifies to the difficulty in defining, let alone managing, organizational culture, the use of cultural change to achieve renewal of public services is being strongly recommended. The Public Service 2000 exercise within the federal government is said to involve ten percent legislative change, 20 percent systems change and 70 percent change to the culture(s) of the bureaucracy. However, the assumption of a simple linear connection between the existence of a strong shared culture based upon vision statements and goals and excellence in organizational performance is not supported by the available research. Both Danny Miller, *The Icarus Paradox* and John P. Kotter and James L. Heskett, *Corporate Cultures and Performance* challenge the popular wisdom that strong cultures automatically lead to strong performance by corporations.[32] They suggest the reverse is also known to occur, that successful performances galvanizes the cultures of organizations. But with success come the dangers of the development of an arrogant, inwardly focused, bureaucratized and coercive culture. Kotter and Heskett argue that "no single cultural formula is associated with long-term performance, especially in an era in which rapid change seems to be the rule."[33] Cultures must be strong and strategically appropriate, but they must also be adaptive. Given the immersion of individual public organizations in the wider political and bureaucratic culture, cultural change within departments and agencies is bound to be slow and uncertain.

Just as the external environment imposes contradictory pressures and demands upon public organizations, their internal processes for the management of change will entail contradictory requirements. Planning will be needed to clarify future directions, to develop a coherent basis for action, to accelerate learning, to exercise whatever control is possible, to develop teamwork and to reassure external stakeholders. The best strategy, however, will not be a detailed plan but a good process. Even corporations facing less complicated environments have reduced their expectations of planning. The prevalent approaches for dealing with increasingly turbulent and unpredictable environments will probably be described most accurately as "adhocracy," "strategic improvisation" and "management by groping along." These terms are meant to imply a conscious combination of systematic planning with continuous adaptive learning. Finding the appropriate balance between muddling through and planning will depend on intimate knowledge of the environment and the internal capabilities of that particular organization, not on any general formula.

NOTES
─────

1. Peter Vaill, *Managing As a Performing Art* (San Francisco: Jossey Bass, 1989), p. 3. Examples of the mammoth literature on organizational change include: John Bryson, *Strategic Planning for Public and Non-Profit Organizations: a Guide to Strengthening and Sustaining Organizational Achievement* (San Francisco: Jossey Bass, 1989); Stanley M. Davis, *Future Perfect* (Don Mills: Addison-Wesley, 1987); Paul L. Harwood, *Adaptive Organizations and People* (Halifax: Institute for Research on Public Policy, 1991); Rosabeth Moss Kanter, Barry A. Stein and Todd D. Jick, *The Challenge of Organizational Change: How Companies Experience It and Leaders Guide It* (New York: Free Press, 1992); Gary D. Kessler, *The Change Riders: Managing the Power of Change* (Don Mills: Addison Wesley, 1991); Jack Koteen, *Strategic Management in Public and Nonprofit Organizations* (New York: Praeger, 1989); Gareth Morgan, *Riding the Waves of Change* (Newbury Park: Sage, 1988); Paul C. Nutt and Robert W. Backoff, *Strategic Management of Public and Third Sector Organizations* (San Francisco: Jossey Bass, 1992); James Brian Quinn, *Strategies for Change: Logical Incrementalism* (Homewood, Ill.: Irwin, 1980); Ralph D. Stacey, *Managing the Unknowable: Strategic Boundaries Between Order and Chaos in Organizations* (San Francisco: Jossey Bass, 1992); Robert Waterman, *The Renewal Factor: How the Best Companies Get and Keep Their Competitive Edge* (New York: Bantam, 1987); and David C. Wilson, *A Strategy of Change: Concepts and Controversies in the Management of Change* (New York: Routledge, 1992).
2. Morgan, *Riding the Waves of Change,* p. 42.
3. See L. Bolman and Terrence Deal, *Modern Approaches to Understanding and Managing Organizations* (San Francisco: Jossey Bass, 1984), p. 44 and W. Scott, *Organizations: Rational, Natural and Open Systems* (Englewood Cliffs, NJ: Prentice-Hall, 1981), p. 65.
4. Nutt and Backoff, *Strategic Management of Public and Third Sector Organizations,* provide a useful review of the techniques available for external assessment. A more theoretical treatment of the topic is

Richard Daft and Karl Weick, "Toward a Model of Organizations as Interpretation System," *Academy of Management Review*, Vol. 9, no. 2 (April 1984), pp. 284-95.

5. See Bryson, *Strategic Planning for Public and Non-Profit Organizations*, chap. 6.

6. Hal G. Rainey, *Understanding and Managing Public Organizations* (San Francisco: Jossey Bass, 1992), p. 42 provides a useful summary of the various classification schemes for environments.

7. Nutt and Backoff, *Strategic Management of Public and Third Sector Organizations*, chap. 3.

8. Daft and Weick, "Toward a Model of Organizations."

9. S. Kiesler and L. Sproull, "Managerial Response to Changing Environments: Perspectives on Problem Sensing from Social Cognition," *Administrative Science Quarterly*, Vol. 27, no. 4 (December 1982), pp. 548-70.

10. Peter J. Frost and Carolyn P. Egri, "The Political Process of Innovation," *Research in Organizational Behaviour*, Vol. 13 (New York: JAI Publications, 1991), pp. 229-95.

11. Herbert Kaufman, *Time, Chance and Organizations: Natural Selection in a Perilous Environment* (Chatham: Chatham House, 1985), chap. 3.

12. Kaufman, *Time, Chance and Organizations*, p. 47.

13. See Gloria Barczak, Charles Smith and David Wilemon, "Managing Large-Scale Organizational Change," *Organizational Dynamics*, Vol. 16, no. 2 (Autumn 1987), pp. 23-35.

14. See the useful synthesis of the literature by Amir Levy, "Second-Order Planned Change: Definition and Conceptualization," *Organizational Dynamics*, Vol. 16, no. 2 (Autumn 1987), pp. 5-20.

15. See the valuable exchange on this point between Henry Mintzberg, "The Design School: Reconsidering the Basic Premises of Strategic Management," *Strategic Management Journal*, Vol. 11, no. 3 (1990), pp. 171-195 and H. Igor Ansoff, "Critique of Henry Mintzberg's 'The Design School'", *Strategic Management Journal*, Vol. 12, no. 4 (1992), pp. 449-66.

16. J.M. Meyer and B. Rowan, "Institutionalized Organizations: Formal Structures as Myth and Ceremony," *American Journal of Sociology*, Vol. 83, no. 2 (April 1977), pp. 346-63.

17. Marshall W. Meyer and L.G. Zucker, *Permanently Failing Organizations* (Beverly Hills: Sage, 1989).

18. Rainey, *Understanding and Managing Public Organizations,* chap. 2 provides a comprehensive review of the normative and empirical literature on the controversy.

19. See Graham T. Allison, "Public and Private Management: Are They Fundamentally Alike in All Unimportant Respects?" in Jay M. Shafritz and Albert C. Hyde (eds.), *Classics of Public Administration* (Pacific Grove, California: Brooks Publishing, 3rd. ed. 1992), pp. 457-75.

20. Short reviews of the literature on the impact of size are found in Barry Bozeman, *Public Management and Policy Analysis* (New York: St. Martin's Press, 1979), pp. 126-30 and Florence Heffron, *Organization Theory and Public Organizations* (Englewood Cliffs, NJ: Prentice-Hall, 1992), pp. 145-49.

21. See Heather Haveman, "Organizational Size and Change: Diversification in the Savings and Loan Industry and Deregulation," *Administrative Science Quarterly,* Vol. 38, no. 1 (March 1993), pp. 20-50.

22. Henry Mintzberg, *The Structuring of Organizations* (Englewood Cliffs, NJ: Prentice Hall, 1983), pp. 230-33.

23. David Zussman and Jak Jabes, *The Vertical Solitude: Managing in the Public Sector* (Halifax: Institute for Research on Public Policy, 1989).

24. Graham White, "Big is different from little: on taking size seriously in the analysis of Canadian governmental institutions," *Canadian Public Administration,* Vol. 33, no. 4 (Winter 1990), pp. 526-50.

25. Sarah J. Freeman and Kim S. Cameron, "Organizational Downsizing: A Convergence and Reorientation Framework," *Organization Science,* Vol. 4, no. 1 (February 1993), pp. 10-29. See also William McKinley, "Decreasing Organizational Size: To Untangle or Not to Untangle," *Academy of Management Review,* Vol. 17, no. 1 (January 1992), pp. 112-23.

26. Bryson, *Strategic Planning for Public and Non Profit Organizations,* chap. 6.

27. An excellent recent treatment of the topic is Jeffrey Pfeffer, *Managing With Power: Politics and Influence in Organizations* (Boston: Harvard Business School Press, 1992).

28. Robert Behn, "Management by Groping Along," *Journal of Policy Analysis and Management* Vol. 7, no. 4 (Fall 1988), pp. 643-63.

29. Peter F. Drucker "The Coming of the New Organization," *Harvard Business Review,* January-February, 1988, pp. 45-53.

30. For the Canadian debate on SOAs see the special issue of *Optimum,* Vol. 22, no. 2 (1991) devoted to the topic. On the overseas experience with executive agencies, useful sources are Jonathan Boston, "Assessing the Performance of Departmental Chief Executives: Perspectives from New Zealand," *Public Administration,* Vol. 70, no. 3 (Autumn 1990), pp. 405-28; Patricia Greer, "The Next Steps Initiative: An Examination of the Agency Framework Documents," *Public Administration,* Vol. 70, no. 1 (Spring, 1992), pp. 90-95; Frank P. Sherwood, "Comprehensive Government Reform in New Zealand," *The Public Manager,* Vol. 21, no. 1 (Spring 1992), pp. 20-24; Enid Wistrich "Managing Sub-National Government in New Zealand," *Public Money and Management,* Vol. 12, no. 4 (October-December, 1992), pp. 25-29; and Enid Wistrich, "Restructuring Government New Zealand Style," *Public Administration,* Vol. 70, no. 1 (Spring 1992), pp. 119-35.

31. Gervase R. Bushe and A. B. Shoni *Parallel Learning Structures: Increasing Innovation in Bureaucracies,* (Don Mills: Addison-Wesley, 1991).

32. James P. Kotter and James L. Heskett, *Corporate Cultures and Performance* (Boston Mass.: Harvard Business School Press, 1992) and Danny Miller, *The Icarus Paradox: How Exceptional Companies Bring About Their Own Downfall* (New York: Harper Collins, 1990).

33. Kotter and Heskett, *Corporate Cultures and Performance,* p. 31.

COMMENTS ON

PAUL THOMAS' PAPER

Paul Thomas, along with his colleague Benjamin Levin, is in the midst of a comprehensive study of how four organizations respond to changes in their external environments. I am quite sure that the ultimate product of this study will be a major book. The paper he presented at this conference is a preliminary look at his findings, a way station on the road to this destination. Thus, I see my responsibility as reacting to this paper in a way that will add value to the book.

Briefly, Thomas did what he calls partnership research in four large organizations, three in the public sector (Agriculture Canada, the Winnipeg Health Sciences Centre and the Seven Oaks School division in suburban Winnipeg), and one in the private sector (Investors Group, a financial services company headquartered in Winnipeg). In partnership research, the organization being studied is involved in the definition of the project and reviews the findings at several points; it is thus a hybrid of social science inquiry and management consultation. The research was intended to help us understand how these organizations studied and interpreted their external environments, and how this environmental analysis affected their agendas.

The research was motivated by, and in some measure attempts to test, the theories in two areas of the management literature. The first is the primarily normative discussion of environmental scanning and strategic planning developed within the field referred to initially as "business policy," and now more frequently as "strategic management." The second is the study of organizational change, which is one of the key topics in the field of macro-organizational behaviour (that is, the study of organizations as entities, as distinct from micro-organizational behaviour, the study of individual behaviour within organizations). As the theme of accelerating environmental change has grown increasingly popular, one could argue that the study of organizational change has come to dominate the field.

Thomas, by training a political scientist, is to be congratulated for having the energy to immerse himself in an entirely new field to undertake this study. His efforts are part of a growing recognition by students of public management, most of whom were trained as either political scientists or economists, that, ultimately, the public sector consists of organizations. Progress can be made by applying the insights of those who have systematically studied organizations, even when, as is usually the case for researchers located in business schools, the organizations studied are in the private sector.

At this stage, Thomas presents four key findings. *First,* normative rational planning models have limited applicability to real organizations, because of the models' formality and complexity, and because of the cognitive and experiential biases of organizational actors. *Second,* urgent operational matters, crisis-management or fire-fighting, tend to crowd strategic planning off the decision-making agenda. *Third,* there was a real difference between the three public sector organizations and one private sector firm, because the latter had a clearer objective, a more refined strategic planning process and stronger central control. *Fourth,* all three public sector organizations were practicing what Robert Behn of Duke University calls Management By Groping Along (MBGA), namely the establishment of a general goal for the organization, and the use of experimentation and adaptation in pursuit of that goal.

These findings all seem consistent with the more recent literature in the field, particularly Behn's MBGA paradigm. Undoubtedly, this cursory statement of Thomas's tentative conclusions misses the subtlety and richness that a book would present. When writing his book and freed from the space constraints of a paper, there are a number of suggestions I would make to Thomas to allow him to present his data as convincingly as possible. In the literature review, he should clearly present the hypotheses to be tested against the case studies. The methodology should be described in more detail than in the paper, and compared with various other social scientific methodologies, such as ethnographic research, participant-observer studies and action research. Initially, each case study should be presented on its own, and each should detail the organization's formal or informal planning system, the key external events and management decisions during the study period, and the relationship, if any, between planning systems and decisions. After presenting each case study, the book should then present a comparative analysis of all four, indicating whether or not they support the hypotheses developed in the literature and comparing the four cases on numerous dimensions. In my own comparative case research, I have made extensive use of tables listing down the rows every conceivable characteristic or hypothesis and across the columns each case studied.[1] I find these tables an extremely helpful way of organizing my thinking and writing.

While it is perhaps premature to characterize the overall thrust of Thomas's work based on a preliminary paper, he does make some statements which suggest that he is, in terms of the dichotomy developed by the British intellectual historian, Isaiah Berlin, a fox rather than a hedgehog, that is, a person who sees a diversity of phenomena rather than a single central vision.[2] For example, he criticizes the recipe-book formula for organizational change in recent management best sellers:

> ... development of an external orientation, incorporating foresight into decision-making, decentralization and delayering, the removal of bureaucratic rules, reliance upon a strong, shared culture to achieve unity of purpose, the development of the competencies of individual employees and their empowerment and the encouragement of ongoing organizational learning.[3]

While any formula can be stretched to the breaking point, the cases I have studied convince me that some major environmental trends are now having an impact on both public and private sector organizations in ways that support the aforementioned formula. I will conclude with two examples. Information technology has already made obsolete a large number of white- or pink-collar jobs (for example, the virtual elimination of receptionists by E-mail in the last five years) and has provided front-line workers with access to much of the organization's data base and senior managers with real-time information about front-line performance. This has enabled front-line workers to take more initiative in service provision and to restructure their jobs in ways that both improve customer service and increase their own satisfaction. An unavoidable consequence is delayering, the reduction in middle management positions as information flows directly between the front lines and head office.

Global competition in the private sector and the debt burden in the public sector have reduced the availability of slack resources within organizations. In both sectors, waste and inefficiency can no longer be tolerated, which dictates a sharp break from the past by developing more focussed strategies, reducing internal cross-subsidization, and instituting efficiency-oriented budgeting and human resources practices.

One implication of the reduction in public sector slack speaks to a key issue considered at this conference, namely whether the main client of the public service is the citizen across the counter or the minister in Ottawa. In many instances, serving ministers in Ottawa has meant providing perks for ministers, rewards to friends for political loyalty, and cross-subsidy to groups deemed to be politically worthy. I would predict that these uses of organizational slack will diminish as the organizational slack itself disappears. A key harbinger of this trend is the wave of national opprobrium and revulsion, if not nausea, Senators provoked in June 1993 by voting themselves (but later rescinding) a $6,000 increase in their expense allowances. Politicians will begin to discover that their political survival depends on understanding public needs, so that there is much less of a dichotomy between serving the public and serving the politician. Isn't that what representative democracy is all about, anyway?

1. Sandford F. Borins with Lee T. Brown, *Investments in Failure: Five Government Corporations that Cost the Canadian Taxpayer Billions* (Toronto: Methuen, 1986).
2. Isaiah Berlin, *The Hedgehog and the Fox: An Essay on Tolstoy's View of History* (New York: New American Library, 1954).
3. Paul Thomas, "Coping with Change: How Public and Private Organizations Read and Respond to Turbulent External Environments," this volume, p. 54-55.

SUMMARY OF DISCUSSION

One participant suggested to Paul Thomas that sometimes we mistake a fad for a long-term trend. Given this, how can we be certain that change is identical to progress? What kinds of criteria can we use? Thomas responded that the short-term pressures governments face make it difficult for them to capture and interpret the changes affecting the environment in which they operate. He added that the most dramatic type of change takes place after a crisis or change in leadership; but since organizations and individuals cherish stability, change represents a threat.

Ted Gaebler commented that many reports show that up to 60 percent of those within an organization resist changes that affect their way of working. Since there is no question that governments are being forced to change, the question is how can we help them to change in a positive manner? How can we help them overcome inertia and find the momentum to change? He added that we need to encourage sources inside government to link up with sources outside government in order to facilitate change. Governments need to learn an important lesson from the private sector, namely that the private sector frequently fails its way to success.

One participant suggested that we all should accept the fact that governments must change; however, we have not sufficiently addressed the related issue of changing the mentality of citizens. The participant added that, when the private sector feels threatened, it initiates change. Can we imagine that the public sector might feel threatened and if so, what would happen? Gaebler said that internal changes can be brought on by a sense of pride. When governments try to change on the basis of pride, it is because they are able to recognize a relationship between their own energies and the end product. People in government have difficulty responding to the question, "What is good government to the people in government?" Gaebler concluded that we need to encourage a change in mindset before this question can be answered.

Another participant suggested that as we further examine change in government we will discover that reform of the bureaucracy and parliamentary structure is what will bring us the change we want at a price we can afford.

Reshaping the Management of Government: The Next Steps Initiative in the United Kingdom

B I L L   J E N K I N S   A N D   A N D R E W   G R A Y

RESHAPING THE MANAGEMENT OF GOVERNMENT:

THE NEXT STEPS INITIATIVE IN THE

UNITED KINGDOM

Within the Next Steps initiative, the emphasis has been on releasing the initiative and energies of middle managers and staff. Managers have been given clearer strategic direction but more freedom to achieve quality results in ways they know will work for customers in their business.[1]

The business of government now, and probably all this century, has been far more tangled and vexatious than running a private sector company of any size simply because Government is the sump into which all the impossible problems ultimately fall.[2]

The year 1993 has been a rough one for the pugnacious British Home Secretary, Kenneth Clarke. After the management of one of Her Majesty's prisons was awarded to a private contractor, Group 4, as part of the government's "market testing" initiative, a number of remand prisoners escaped from Group 4's care and another died while in its charge. Questions were duly asked in the House of Commons and it was rumoured that Group 4's management held emergency meetings to decide whether it should be in this business at all. In the event it decided to remain.

All this coincided with Clarke's announcement of what he described as "the most important reforms of the UK police service for 30 years" (a regime of decentralized management by objectives) and, less trumpeted but no less significant, the metamorphosis on April 1, 1993 of the Prison Service as a Next Steps executive agency, under Derek Lewis, a chief executive with an excellent track record in commercial management but no experience, one way or the other, of prisons.[3]

These examples illustrate crucial aspects of the changing world of public sector management in the United Kingdom. In a wide range of services the talk is now of delegated budgets, targets, performance, audit, contracts and purchaser/provider relationships as the new managerialism takes hold.[4] The causes and consequences of these important changes in the relationships among politicians, public service managers and clients are only now being explored.[5] What is clear, however, is that they are part of an international fashion followed in countries as varied as Australia, New Zealand and the United States.[6]

This paper examines only one, but an important, part of this management revolution in the UK, namely the genesis and development of departmental executive agencies under a program known as the Next Steps. The description and analysis will centre on changes in the civil service, especially the management of ministerial departments, and the relationship of these departments with central government organizations such as the Treasury. The aim is to explain how a major program of political and administrative change was initiated and implemented and to raise questions about the strengths and weaknesses of the Next Steps initiative and the assumptions on which it and other strands of the "new public management" are based.

After an opening section on the origins and development of the Next Steps initiative, the paper focusses more closely on the way agencies are created and on the evolving relationships between the centre of UK government, ministerial departments and agencies and Parliament. This is followed by a discussion of agency performance, effectiveness and relationships with clients and customers, a discussion of implications and issues and a final reflective conclusion.

THE NEXT STEPS INITIATIVE: GENESIS AND DEVELOPMENT

By the late 1970s, the received wisdom both within and outside the UK civil service was that previous attempts to change the management of government had been too ambitious and imprecisely focussed. Moreover, management was neglected, financial control weak and many, if not most, government activities were inefficient.[7] When Margaret Thatcher became Prime Minister in 1979, she clearly shared this view and was convinced that the size of the public sector, especially public expenditure, needed to be reduced as part of a primary concern with macro-economic management. These concerns remain under John Major. Thus management initiatives are important only as far as they contribute to public expenditure control.[8]

The story of early attempts in the 1980s to change the management of the UK civil service are well described elsewhere.[9] Briefly, these included the creation in 1979 of the Prime Minister's Efficiency Unit and the launch in 1982 of the Financial Management Initiative (FMI). Headed by a succession of industrialists and one retired civil servant, the Unit has been a catalyst for initiating managerial change in government through its program of departmental efficiency scrutinies. In the mind of Lord Rayner (its first head and senior executive of the British retailer, Marks & Spencer), its task was not only to detect and drive out waste but also to change the culture of the civil service by making good management a valued and well rewarded activity.

The FMI promulgated Rayner's values on a much broader scale. Its instruments have been delegated budgets, the creation of information systems and a regime of accountable management under which managers were given a certain amount of operational freedom so long as they met resource and performance targets.[10]

By the late 1980s sections of opinion in Whitehall were concerned that progress in the FMI and elsewhere was not as fast and substantial as required. Indeed, there was a suspicion that it was being blocked in some quarters. As a result the Efficiency Unit, then headed by Sir Robin Ibbs, formerly of ICI, carried out an evaluation of the reforms. As with all efficiency scrutinies, the study was conducted in 90 working days, during which the team talked to ministers, permanent secretaries and former civil servants. They also visited regional and local offices of departments and a number of private sector organizations.

In its report, *Improving Management in Government: the Next Steps,*[11] the team claimed that:

- the civil service was too large to manage as a single organization;
- ministerial overload diverted attention from management matters;
- the freedom of middle managers was being frustrated by hierarchical controls; and
- there was little emphasis on the achievement of results.

These fundamental problems demanded radical changes in the delivery of government services, in the departments themselves and at the centre of government. Departments needed to focus on the work to be done and ways in which to sustain continuous improvement in the delivery of policy and services. The team's principal proposal was the designation of discrete operational areas of activity and the establishment of departmental executive agencies. Each was to be headed by a chief executive who would be free, within policy and resources frameworks set by departments, to manage their "businesses." Ministerial accountability would remain but would not stretch to the detail of management.

It is important to note that the focus of the report was on government in general rather than simply the civil service in particular. This may have been forgotten as events proceeded. However, even though its evidence and analysis were somewhat limited, its prescription of agencies caught the mood of Thatcher and her colleagues. Perhaps inevitably, there was considerable resistance to its findings in Whitehall. This was responsible in part for a year's delay before Thatcher announced to the House of Commons in February 1988 that the report's major recommendations had been accepted.[12] From then on the executive or service delivery functions of government would be, to the greatest extent practicable, carried out by "Next Steps" agencies and, to this end, the implementation of the program would be directed by a senior level project manager with the full backing of the Prime Minister.

The Development of Agencies 1988-91

Seasoned observers of UK government responded to the Prime Minister's announcement with a degree of cynicism. True, the Rayner efficiency program and the FMI had been implemented more successfully than many expected, but the track record of lasting structural change in Whitehall was poor. Given the experience of the nationalized industries (e.g., coal, steel, railways), the idea of ministers adopting an "arms length" approach to important parts of their departmental empire seemed especially optimistic.

Such a reaction appears to have been confounded by the implementation of the Next Steps. In particular, the appointment of a project manager, initially Peter Kemp (from the Treasury) may be an object lesson in the management of change in Whitehall.[13] Aided by a small group of officials attached to the Cabinet Office (the Next Steps Team), Kemp set out to both prod and encourage departments to offer up agency candidates. The strategy was not only to promote a management environment in which Next Steps could flourish but also to throw grit into the civil service machine and force departments to justify their activities. "If we are to achieve permanent change we must question, question, question what we are doing and continually seek for ways of improving it."[14]

The initial pace of agency creation (1988-89) was steady rather than spectacular. By the summer of 1989, eight agencies had been created, including the Vehicle Inspectorate (Department of Transport), HMSO (HM Treasury) and the Civil Service College (Office of the Minister for the Civil Service). Many of these were almost already *de facto* agencies with well defined businesses and a commercial outlook. Moreover, the project team met with a mixed reaction in Whitehall. Some departments, already organized on federal lines (e.g., Employment) found little difficulty in adapting to agencies, and others welcomed the opportunity to take a road often urged on them by powerful interest groups within a department (e.g., Social Security). In other cases, however, there was resistance to reorganizing departmental machinery yet again and upsetting established interests and only token candidates were put up.

Nevertheless, the project team persevered and the pace quickened. In 1990 the initiative was described by the House of Commons Treasury and Civil Service Select Committee as "the most ambitious attempt at civil service reform in the 20th century"[15] and in 1991 the Committee noted the "impressive speed of developments."[16] However, questions were raised about interference in agency managerial freedoms by parent departments and Treasury controls over framework documents and managerial regimes.

Partly to answer these questions, a second Efficiency Unit investigation was initiated. Its report, *Making the Most of the Next Steps,*[17] looked especially at departmental-agency relationships. It concluded that, although there was much to be praised, there was considerable room for improvement if the Next Steps ideals were to be realized. It recommended the development of a more "shared vision" of what an agency was for and a more hands-off regime for both sponsoring departments and the centre (especially the Treasury) to allow further progress in delegating freedoms. The government broadly accepted these conclusions although it noted that "agencies" delegations and flexibilities can be enlarged as their track record of performance is established, *provided that the essential controls on public expenditure are not jeopardised"* (emphasis added).[18]

Agencies, Consumers and Markets 1991-93

In November 1990 Thatcher resigned as Prime Minister and was succeeded by John Major. Two and a half years and one general election later the Next Steps program continues apace. As of April 1993, the list of agencies totals 89, employing over 260,000 civil servants, nearly two-thirds of the total (see Appendix A). More recent inclusions range from the Prison Service and the Child Support Agency to the Royal Parks and the Army Base Repair Agency. Numbers of employees now range from the 64,215 in the Social Security Benefits Agency to the 25 in the Wilton Park Conference Centre. There are also 19 further candidates identified for agency status (see Appendix B). The current plan of the Next Steps team is to identify all agency candidates by the end of 1993 and to launch them by April 1995. Agencies will then embrace roughly 75 percent of civil service personnel and, having achieved its task, the Next Steps team (in its present form) will probably disband.

Yet while there has been continuity over the past two years there have also been important changes in the political environment and the internal management of the initiative. The former derives at least in part from the change of prime minister. Major, it is said, cares about the public services. His personal initiative, the Citizen's Charter (Cm. 1599, 1991), aims to provide "a revolution in public services" by emphasizing and raising the quality of service delivery. All government departments, the national health service and bodies such as the railways and the privatized utilities (e.g., telecommunications, electricity, gas and water) are included and the program is managed by the Citizen's Charter Unit in the Cabinet Office and a prime ministerial adviser drawn from the private sector. Under this guidance, organizations are encouraged to produce their own charters setting out service targets and methods of redress. The charter initiative also emphasizes prompt service, openness, customer research and a stronger voice for citizens (Cm. 2101, 1992).

Next Steps agencies which deal directly with the public are seen as "vehicles for the delivery of the charter."[19] Moreover, they are now also subject to the new regime of "market testing" which has emerged from a long standing commitment by the government to compulsory competitive tendering in public services. First tried out in the national health service and local government (e.g., in catering, office cleaning, and estate maintenance), it is now being extended more widely in the public sector, including the civil service, following the government White Paper, *Competing for Quality* (Cm. 1730, 1991). The government's argument is that the further improvement of public services requires a substantial of expansion of competition. All government departments and agencies have therefore been required to apply market testing to new areas of their operations and to set targets for a proportion of activities exposed in this way. New areas to be tested cover a wide range of activities ranging from support services (e.g., cleaning and catering) to "areas closer to the heart of government."[20] Initial reports indicate the testing of services as varied as milk hygiene enforcement (Ministry of Agriculture) through court escort services for prisoners (Home Office) to the Library of HM Treasury (Cm. 2101, 1992, pp. 60-64). In all this the claim is that competitive tendering or market testing is a proven success in raising quality and saving money. For a government with a large public sector borrowing requirement, the attractions are obvious.

One organizational consequence of John Major's surprise election victory in April 1992 was the creation of a new ministry, the Office of Public Service and Science (OPSS), headed by a minister of cabinet rank. In encompassing the Efficiency Unit, Next Steps, the Citizen's Charter and the market testing program, the new ministry has responsibility for all the current major managerial initiatives in British central government (HC. 390-i, 1992-3). The initial moves of the first minster, William Waldegrave, however, were not the most auspicious. He appeared to engineer the removal of his permanent secretary, Sir Peter Kemp, who had steered Next Steps program through its formative years. It was said that Sir Peter's skills were inappropriate for the new job in the enlarged department.[21] Sir Peter therefore took early retirement and in his place a more traditional career grade civil servant Richard

Mottram was appointed.

Management reform in UK central government is therefore current-ly moving along three related tracks: Next Steps agencies, the Citizen's Charter and market testing. How far these are complimentary or con-flicting is something that will be examined later. For the moment, how-ever, we turn to explore the dynamics of agency creation and operation.

THE CENTRE, DEPARTMENTS AND AGENCIES

The Management of Change

Framed and displayed in the office of Lord Rayner, Thatcher's first efficiency adviser, hung the following:

> It must be considered that there is nothing more perilous to conduct or more uncertain in its success than to take the lead in a new order of things. For the reformer has enemies in all those who profit by the old order, and only lukewarm defenders in all who would profit by the new. (N. Machiavelli, *The Prince*).

The passage contains self-evident but important truths for anyone seeking to implement organizational change. Prior to 1979, the track record of change management in UK central government was poor. Against this the history of the Efficiency Unit, the Financial Management Initiative and now Next Steps indicates that extensive change is possible in large scale public sector organizations. But, this history suggests also that success depends on a number of preconditions: a dedicated band of change agents, high level support or political clout for their activities, and an incremental style of management that attempts to work with the grain of public sector organizations rather than against it.

The approach of the Next Steps Team under Peter Kemp (1988-92) exemplifies all of these factors.[22] The program involved a number of major players at the centre of UK government: the Next Steps Team, the Treasury (in various guises) and individuals in the Cabinet Office, including Sir Robin Butler, Cabinet Secretary and Head of the UK Home Civil Service. This administrative drive was (and continues to be) reinforced, moreover, by a high level political interest in developments, first through Thatcher and later through John Major, a factor vital in dealing with ministers who may not ordinarily be interested in management change.

The Next Steps team's major task was to select, launch and sustain individual agencies while developing the momentum of the program as a whole. Kemp and his unit did this by a mixture of persistence (harrying departments until they conformed with the program) and persuasion (attempting to demonstrate to both departments and potential agencies the benefits that might flow from agency status). This strategy of "logical incrementalism"[23] can be contrasted sharply with earlier comprehensive attempts in the 1960s and 1970s to effect uniform change throughout the civil service. As Kemp never tired of pointing out, he saw the civil service as a heterogenous rather than a homogenous entity. Therefore, there was no one single agency model; rather, arrangements depended on the task performed and the environment operated in. To the question "what is an agency?" there is, therefore, no one answer.[24] Next Steps represents in part a philosophy and in part an organizational form and set of procedures. How these take effect, however, varies from case to case.

The Making of an Agency

Under the Next Steps program up to 1992, central departments were urged to study their activities and to propose agency candidates. Following this the Next Steps Unit and the department met with the Treasury to examine whether the activities identified should be privatized, their work contracted out or dispensed with altogether (HC. 348, 1989, pp. 50-57). If the answers to these questions were negative, then a decision would be made as to whether the agency form was appropriate. Important factors influencing this outcome included the political sensitivity of the activity and whether the creation of an agency would improve the quality of management and service. If the analysis remained favourable, work would move on to the design of a policy and resources framework, within which the agency would operate, and the appointment of the chief executive.

Agencies have been, therefore, a choice *after* the privatization option has been rejected, although this option may be reconsidered, e.g., after a three year review. Agencies thus remain *departmental* organizations, with the chief executive accountable to the minister and the minister in turn accountable to Parliament, and their employees retain the status of civil servants, although their pay and conditions may vary (see below).

More recently, however, the selection procedure has been altered. Since April 1992, all agency candidates have been considered for market testing with the possibility that, if an in-house bid was successful, then an agency form would be an option. However, the majority of agencies were established prior to this date.

Frameworks, Targets and Chief Executives

A central emphasis of the original Efficiency Unit report (1988) was that agencies should be established in a way that facilitated managerial energy and freedoms. It was therefore proposed that each agency have its own policy and resources framework and be headed by a chief executive. This formula has been closely followed as the agency initiative has proceeded.

The framework document is not a corporate plan, nor is it a legal document in contract law, although some argue that this should now take effect.[25] Rather, framework documents set out the parameters in which the agency is to be managed. Although they differ in content as well as presentation,[26] they all contain:

- an outline of the agency's objectives and targets against which performance can be measured;
- details of the financial and human resource management frameworks (see below); and
- details of department-agency relations.

The document emerges after negotiations between the Next Steps Unit, the Treasury and the parent department and is reviewed after three years. Certain changes, e.g., in targets, can be made at any time.

The issue of targets is fundamentally important in illustrating the departmental and wider political context of agencies. Although technically set by ministers, targets are proposed in practice by chief executives and then negotiated. However, targets can be altered by ministers as they wish or set to fit political circumstances. Faced with such ministerial fiat, chief executives have few options: "At the end of the day Chief Executives are operating under discipline and they actually have the choice of doing one of two things. They can buckle down and do what the minister has asked them to do; or they can resign."[27]

But who are the chief executives, how are they appointed and how are they rewarded? In the early days most chief executives were drawn from inside the civil service and posts were not necessarily openly advertised. However, pressed on by the Treasury and Civil Service Select Committee, most chief executive posts (other than possibly sensitive areas such as defence) are now openly advertised and of the 61 recruited by open competition 32 have come from outside the civil service from a variety of backgrounds including local government, the NHS and the private sector.[28] These individuals are on fixed term contracts and salaries that have performance related elements linked to agency targets. They also, in theory at least, have direct access to ministers.

The Internal Management of Agencies: Finance and Human Resources

One of the most frequent complaints of managers in the UK civil service has been of the hierarchical financial regimes in which they had to operate. Purchasing, appointing temporary staff and even painting the office often seemed impossible without reference to principal finance officers. More fundamentally, the annuality limits of the budget and controls over capital investment decisions hampered efficiency and effectiveness. The Financial Management Initiative with its philosophy of accountable management was intended to move departments from this position and the Next Steps to take these changes in delegation and financial freedom even further.

Often, the enemy has been seen as the Treasury with its obsession with "running costs" and with holding down spending irrespective of consequences. Against this, the Treasury's official position is that it has always been keen to negotiate realistic financial freedoms for agencies, as long as these are compatible with public expenditure policy.[29] What is important for the Treasury is the nature of an agency's task or business and how robust its financial management systems are. In terms of yielding freedoms, agencies vary greatly and will be treated accordingly.

This difference between types of agencies was central to the second Efficiency Unit report (1991). This emphasized that agency tasks ranged from those fundamental to mainstream policy (e.g., the Employment Service) to those not linked to any of the main objectives of the Department (e.g., HMSO, the Historic Royal Palaces).[30]

These differences are crucial in shaping the management regimes negotiated in framework documents. Twelve agencies, for example, are now treated as "trading funds," i.e., as commercial businesses with freedoms over capital investment and carry over procedures. Such bodies are those with identifiable businesses and products (e.g., HMSO, the Royal Mint, and the Vehicle Inspectorate). However, if some other agencies are moving in this direction, it is clear that many, such as the Social Security Benefits Agency, provide functions that will probably never be part of such a regime.[31] As a consequence, their freedoms are likely to remain limited.

However, financial freedoms are not the only management systems of importance. Encouraged by the Treasury's policy of local rather than national pay bargaining, agencies are developing their own pay and personnel management regimes (e.g., HMSO and the Royal Mint). Further, from April 1994, all agencies with over 2,000 staff will have responsibility for their own pay bargaining. The Treasury has also urged that all new systems link pay with performance.[32] Meanwhile, in the wider field of human resource and personnel management, the Civil Service (Management Functions) Act, passed in December 1992, has given scope for the Treasury to delegate to agencies powers to alter the terms and conditions of staff without further reference to the centre. This short piece of legislation could have wide and significant consequences.

AGENCIES, CLIENTS AND EFFECTIVENESS

Regimes of Performance and Efficiency

It is perhaps too easy to criticize systems of targets and results. As the literature of performance indicators demonstrates, well designed systems have the capacity to improve organizational and management performance.[33] However, one must also be aware of the role of information in the politics of organizations and the fact that the criteria of good design and systems of measurements may themselves be the outcome of political debate, a fact well established in the world of policy evaluation and audit.[34]

As with the Financial Management Initiative (FMI) before it, the Next Steps program assumes that good management requires a discipline of targets both to focus and motivate managers and to assess performance. This is consistent with the wider use of performance indicators in the public expenditure review process and in the financial regimes that departments can negotiate with the Treasury.[35] As we have already noted above, agency targets are officially set by ministers:

> Each agency is set clear objectives and demanding targets by its Minister, covering key aspects of its business including quality of service, financial performance and efficiency. Within this strategic framework, responsibility for the management of the operation, and the freedom and flexibility to manage effectively and efficiently, is vested in the Chief Executive.[36]

In reality, the process is more complex than this, with chief executives suggesting to ministers programs of targets which ministers may or may not accept. The Treasury also takes a close interest, not least since pressure on targets may be one way of squeezing budgets or pressurising ministers to produce savings. Thus, targets may be the result of political negotiation both within departments and between departments and the centre. This emphasizes the way chief executives operate within the paradigm of politics as much as that of managerial efficiency.

But how are targets designed, what do they tell us and how have agencies "measured up" to them? In 1991, the Treasury submitted a paper to the Treasury and Civil Service Select Committee entitled *Executive Agencies – Setting Targets and Measuring Performance: A Guide* (HC. 496 1990-1, Appendix 11). This paper was written by a civil servant, Bill St Clair, formerly the head of the Treasury's work on policy evaluation. The guide, which was not mandatory, suggested a sequence of "objectives, output and performance measures and then targets." It recommended that only a handful of "key targets" be selected to reflect financial performance, output, quality of service and efficiency, that they be part of the "corporate planning process" and be linked as far as possible to policy evaluation. However, the paper recognized that "output" and "quality of service" posed particular measurement problems and that a service "may need to be judged through sample peer group reviews or the customers' own views."[37]

How far the realities of agency target setting measures up to the Treasury guidelines is difficult to judge. In terms of published data, the categories of *Quality of Service, Financial, Efficiency* and *Throughput* used in the Next Steps Annual Reports (e.g., Cm. 2111, 1992, pp. 96-7) come with a health warning that targets are tailored specifically for each agency and that categorizations are approximate. However, specific examinations of individual agencies show the predominance of financial (e.g., staying in budget or breaking even) or turnover targets (e.g., 90 percent of driving licences to be issued within thirteen days, passport applications to be processed within an average of nine working days).

Such efforts should not be belittled. The regime acts as a focus and a discipline for those running the organization while offering a guide to agency clients and others of what can be expected. Of course, not all agencies meet their targets (Cm. 2111, 1992, pp. 5-7). This has consequences for both chief executives' pay and the assessment of the management regime (although it might also tell us about ministerial fiats). However, how far the "success" of agencies can be assessed from studies of targets remains an open question. Current target data says little of agency impact and value for money. Similarly, "quality" defined as "quality of service" constitutes a rather narrow perspective when neither the product of the service itself nor the consequences of activities is assessed.

What the current regimes of agency targets indicate, therefore, is a greater commitment to more structured management processes and an attempt to assess performance over time. They say little of the impact of agency activities or strategic direction. Perhaps these are reserved for agency business plans (not always published) or the policy core of the parent department. However, if the latter is the case, it challenges the assumption made by Next Steps architects that administration and policy can be separated clearly.[38] It also hints at the wider implications which the development of executive agencies may have had for the management of central government in Britain. Some of these are discussed in the following section.

IMPLICATIONS

At one level the Next Steps might be seen as an interesting and probably successful example of structural reform in government, success being measured strictly in terms of its implementation. What is clear from the reports of the Treasury and Civil Service Select Committee and the academic literature, however, is that any assessment of the initiative must also deal with a range of wider issues including the federalising of the civil service, public accountability and the changing machinery of government.

A federated civil service?

The original Efficiency Unit report (1988) stated that the British civil service was too large to manage as one unit. Yet various writers would question whether there ever was an effective unitary management.[39] British government is highly differentiated both across and within departments. The architects of Next Steps acknowledged this and the creation of agencies has reinforced the "federal" nature both of departments and of government as a whole.[40] However, as the changes move beyond structure to embrace both personnel regimes and human resources management, federalization becomes a more significant issue. As the First Division Association (the body representing senior ranks of the UK civil service) recently noted, the new climate is characterized by "a shift away from a uniform, centralized system of civil service pay and conditions" and its replacement by "legislation enabling divergent departmental and agency recruitment practices, and the use of short term contracts for civil servants" (First Division Association in HC. 390, 1992-3). Such moves are therefore seen, especially by civil service unions, as threatening the nature of the civil service, in particular its career structure (e.g., limiting transferability) and neutrality (e.g., the effects of contracts).[41]

Management freedoms

Such moves may be seen as inevitable, and even necessary and progressive as part of a wider decentralization of government in which freedoms are yielded to managers and responsibility for service delivery is pushed closer to citizens. In this sense it is consistent with changes elsewhere in British government, such as in the local management of schools and the creation of hospital trusts. However, as many of the discussions on decentralization indicate, true "freedom" to manage demands the centre or organizations yield power. Thus, to be effective, decentralized management must be a *political* as much as an *organizational* strategy.[42]

Previous studies of the Financial Management Initiative have demonstrated the limits of such moves. As one manager once told us, his view of the FMI changes was that they resulted in "a little bit of freedom and a lot of grief."[43] Whether the Next Steps have provided more substantive freedom is unclear. Some studies indicate that lower level agency managers still often find themselves in this bind.[44] There are also other indications that, in spite of Treasury protestations, the yielding of freedoms remains limited (Efficiency Unit, 1991, para. 2.15).

Public accountability

Yet how far do such freedoms and their development threaten traditional public sector accountability? How far is the risk taking, entrepreneurial world of devolved government compatible with detailed legislative scrutiny, audit and accountability? For administrative theorists and practising politicians, the problem starts with the fact that while the term "accountability" is in universal currency it is often defined in very different way.[45] This has not helped the clarification of agency accountability to Parliament, especially with regard to the position of chief executives. This issue has been pursued by successive Parliamentary Select Committee inquiries (HC. 348, 1988-9; HC. 481, 1989-90; HC. 496, 1990-91) and by individual MPs. Ministers are accountable to parliament for the activities of their departments and of the agencies within, yet chief executives are responsible for agency operations. At issue is what mechanisms and powers Parliament has to scrutinize the agencies. At one level this matter may seem trivial. However, the fundamental issue at stake here is that between accountability and managerial freedom. One view is that detailed scrutiny can only inhibit innovation. The response is that scrutiny is essential to the enhancement of good and responsible government.

The machinery of government

The agency initiative therefore has the potential to redefine some of the wider processes of UK Parliamentary government. However, it may also effect the machinery of government itself. This arises from the fact that for most, if not all, departments the creation of agencies reduces the size of the departmental core. This is very much in line with the original aim of agencies delivering services and small departmental central cores focussing on policy work and the strategic frameworks in which agencies operate (Efficiency Unit, 1988).

These core-agency relationships were the focus of the second Efficiency Unit Report (1991). This report sought to aid the empowerment of agency chief executives and to reappraise the role, organization and size of departments. Its thrust was that, based on private sector experience, the core of departments should be reduced in size and functions pushed out to agencies themselves (e.g., the holding company model). It was also recommended that central departments, particularly the Treasury, adopted a more "hands off" approach to management.

At present, in the era of citizen's charters and market testing, the second Efficiency Unit Report (1991) appears to have been shunted into a siding. However, its analysis implies that as agencies are created and departments change so in turn will the role of ministers both as heads of department as members of Cabinet. If ministers are to retain only "arms length" control over agencies and if their department comprises agencies and a small policy core, what is the role of ministers? Indeed will some ministries really be needed? Collectively, will cabinet composition and functions change and, in turn, will a different type of politician be required? At present, such questions are rarely articulated, let alone addressed, yet they would seem of fundamental importance as Next Steps agencies begin to redefine the architecture of the British state.[46]

Evidence of Agency Success

Any assessment of agency success can be at present only speculative. This holds for the performance of individual agencies as well as for the initiative as a whole. The Treasury and Civil Service Select Committee's persistent efforts to have Next Steps evaluated (HC. 496, 1990-1, para 35) have been resisted by the government as "premature" (Cm. 1761, 1992, p. 5). The centre's position is that the number of different agencies make any large scale evaluation impractical.

At the level of individual agencies, however, the current policy is to highlight features that indicate how the creation of agencies has led to improved performance and better service to customers. Set out by the Next Steps team, these "developments" cover a variety of agencies and involve widely different examples.[47] They include a "Visitors' Charter" by the Historic Royal Palaces, a "customer service" regime by the Land Registry and a specialist telephone helpline in the Social Security Benefits Agency. There is also evidence of more specific efforts to gauge customer awareness and needs. These mainly take the form of customer surveys (e.g., by the Driving Standards Agency, the Employment Service) but can include also the use of consultative client groups to asses the need for new products and services (e.g., by the Hydrographic Office), customer conferences and seminars (Social Security Contributions Agency) and liaison meetings with consumer organizations (Veterinary Medicines Directorate).

All this is interesting but, inevitably, difficult to assess as external audit of client effectiveness is rarely conducted nor are independent inspectorates involved in these processes. Initiatives are usually agency driven and internally evaluated using external consultants. However, the National Audit Office (NAO) can investigate agencies and has carried out one study (of the Vehicle Inspectorate, one of the original agencies (HC. 249, 1992). Although the NAO's assessment of the Vehicle Inspectorate's progress was favourable, it argued that, without a change in governmental policy, scope for further improvements was limited. In particular, without a relaxation in the restrictions on the Inspectorate's ability to expand its business, the scope for radical improvements would become exhausted and management would find the ability to make progress difficult.[48]

Agencies and the Market: Empowerment of the Citizen?

The previous discussion raises wider questions on an agency's capacity for success especially in the new political climate where the Next Steps initiative has been joined by the Citizen's Charter (Cm. 1599, 1991) and the "Competing for Quality" initiative (Cm. 1730, 1991). The 1990s has seen the rediscovery of the "citizen" by all the main UK political parties. Hence, Labour and Liberal-Democrat politicians point to local government regimes under their control where the focus is on decentralized administration, client choice and mechanisms of local self-determination. There is also much talk of "empowerment," rights and redress and now the post-Maastricht concept of "subsidiarity."

However, as ever, while there may be agreement on the general terms in this debate the nature of specific meanings is open to different interpretations. Thus critiques of Major's charter initiative argue that it has little to do with systems of enforceable rights and much to do with a model of citizen as customer in a market. In this model empowerment emerges from market solutions (e.g., competition), through stronger regulation of monopoly power (e.g., the regulation of privatized monopolies such as gas), or through the creation of quasi-markets where purchasers and providers are split (e.g., the recent national health service reforms).[49] The critics argue that empowerment should involve enforceable rights and increased powers of redress. In this alternative model "empowerment" means the surrender of power by central organizations and political bodies. Anything less is seen as cosmetic and ineffective.[50]

Such seemingly theoretical and definitional problems are important to any examination and assessment of Next Steps in an age of charters and markets. In particular, the importation of the language of the market place (and the meanings it carries) can have important political and administrative implications. As Pollitt has noted, whether one is called customer, client or citizen carries with it different implications and different expectations of what rights and expectations a recipient of service might have.[51]

In the case of Next Steps, identifying an agency's "customer" has never been easy for those running the program. Some agencies clearly have consumers but is the ultimate "customer" the minister? While such questions appear to verge on hair splitting, they are crucial in assessing the freedoms that chief executives and their staffs might have. Wider government policy determines the way agencies relate to clients and policy is a ministerial responsibility. Hence, if government policy is to limit the public sector in size and capacity and to prevent public sector organizations moving into areas of private sector business then the entrepreneurial scope for agencies is *de facto* limited. This is the reason that the Vehicle Inspectorate's activities (discussed above) are constrained and are likely to remain so (HC. 249, 1992). This is also the reason that benefit take up is not an agency target. Such moves may be wholly respectable politically but this political framework constrains and to some extent controls managerial innovation. It also emphasizes policy inconsistencies that are likely to hamper managerial reform.

A similar problem now emerges with regard to market testing especially as this effects agency development. For those formerly responsible for the Next Steps initiative, market testing, while a reasonable policy in itself, is being implemented in such a way as to threaten the internal management of agencies. Hence, in evidence to the Treasury and Civil Service Select Committee, Sir Peter Kemp (former Next Steps project manager) warned that if the implementation of a program of market testing was too hasty it would undermine the motivations of agency senior managers and staff.[52] As Sue Richards has noted there is considerable unease about market testing both amongst UK senior administrators and staff in the agencies. Both the development and the implementation of "market testing" are seen as "stepping across the strategic plans for change in agencies and lowering the morale of agency staff and managers."[53]

At the moment it is probably too early to make firm judgements on the market testing initiative. However, there seems to be clear evidence that most departments are going along with it in a reluctant fashion and that many of the activities offered for market testing are at best peripheral (e.g., typing, messenger services, payroll etc) (Cm. 2101, 1992, pp. 61-64). There is also, unsurprisingly, strong resistance to these developments from civil service unions not least with regard to the conditions of service and rights of employees caught up in the initiative. This resistance has, in turn led to appeals to the Courts under European Community Law and some difficult legal problems for the government. A crucial piece of legislation here is the European Communities Acquired Rights directive implemented in Britain through the Transfer of Undertakings (Protection of Employment) Regulations (known as TUPE). This, it would appear, guarantees the pay and conditions for public sector staff if their work is contracted out to new employees. If this proves to be the case then any savings from "market testing" are likely to be minimal and, at the time of writing, there is considerable political and legal confusion over this issue.[54] Hence, as Richards and Rodrigues point out, while the benefits of market testing remain uncertain[55] the potential costs are high ranging from a loss of morale and motivation of grass root civil servants who view (rightly or wrongly) their jobs as being under threat to an undermining of Agency Chief Executives who consider such developments to be a diversion from the real problems they face and the fundamental need for a more forceful decentralization of control from core departments and HM Treasury to the agencies themselves.[56]

CONCLUSION

Is the Next Steps program an end in itself or the means to a wider objective? Its creators might respond that their aim was to facilitate the better management of government. This, however, demands some analysis of what is meant whether policy and execution can really be separated. The good delivery of bad policy is hardly the measure of a healthy state nor, perhaps, is a system which, while mouthing the language of empowerment, choice and citizen's rights, acts in a consistently centralist way with regard to the making of policy decisions.

It can be argued that the Next Steps has succeeded as a management innovation. Through it a large section of the UK civil service has been structurally changed, possibly on a permanent basis. Organizational cultures have also been altered along with both the rhetoric and processes of management. In some, though perhaps not all, of the agencies real improvements in service delivery have been achieved and organizations have began to relate to clients in a different way. These have been important gains, fulfilling the hopes of those who designed and took forward the Next Steps.

Yet, here are also important criticisms. These include the inadequacy of frameworks and the failure to clarify the role of chief executives or to empower them. Effective frameworks can only be set if there are clear objectives to follow. In many instances (especially in politically sensitive areas) such objectives are either ambiguous, symbolic, token or all three. Perhaps this is a failure of the policy making capacity of government. With regard to chief executives the issue of concern is that government by "contract" in agencies is a one-way relationship from minister to chief executive, where contracts can be altered or redefined in response to crisis or ministerial whim. This can make effective management impossible. Hence the suggestion that contracts should become more formalized and given legal status so that minister-agency relationships can be clearly defined and areas of responsibility and freedom established.[57]

Yet such structural adjustments alone may solve little. A failure of some of the new public management and, indeed, the original creators of Next Steps, is to ignore or downplay the *political* nature of what they suggest (i.e., changes in structure alter the *political* map of organizations and government whether this is intended or not). In this sense, the Next Steps is a political reform not a managerial one. It is foolish to imagine that, in many areas of government, policy and executive work can be split or that better government can be engineered simply through changes in policy delivery. Hence, current reforms overlook the need to:

- improve governmental strategic capacity and direction;
- integrate the initiatives currently in play; and
- recognize that policy making and policy implementation are often inseparably linked.

Perhaps these omissions explain the persistence of the question "next steps to where?"[58] In government such a question may be met with a deafening silence. Strategic analysis has not been a major part of recent developments. True, it was paid lip service in the Financial Management

Initiative and, for a while, the UK Treasury flirted with policy evaluation.[59] However, the strengthening of a strategic capacity and framework has not gone hand in hand with the changes discussed. Rather, these often proceed in a policy vacuum steered by a system that operates through a system of crisis management and blame avoidance.[60]

Moreover, there is a lack of any effective integrating strategy for government activities. Recent policy crises over pit closures, employment and energy policies are the inevitable result. Current management initiatives such as agencies, the Citizen's Charter and market testing are similarly weakly integrated with little in the way of overarching strategy to link them or a mechanism for considering the effects of each program on the others in the short or long term. Nor, as far as one is aware, are there plans for any formal evaluation.

The logic of the new public management encourages and expands this decentralized world, pushing control and responsibility down the government machine (and possibly creating new sub-governments as it proceeds). Yet this raises the question of what integrating mechanisms are required and how the centre needs to be redefined to cope with and manage such changes. The issue of the balance of power between centre and periphery or between governments and sub-governments also needs to be addressed.

Observers of UK local government and the health service have pointed out that, far from empowering local people, recent moves have strengthened the powers of central government and effectively disenfranchised citizens by fragmenting mechanisms of a voice (e.g., in health, education, housing, and social services). The issue of reduced accountability in these new systems has also been raised.[61] The response to this is that layers of bureaucracy have been removed and the new arrangements should be seen as democratic, flexible and responsive.

A similar view may be taken of changes described in this paper, namely that, while many recent management initiatives in UK central government have advanced the cause of decentralization and empowerment, they have not addressed the *political* and *machinery of government* changes required to facilitate this. As a consequence, the effects of what has so far been achieved are limited and likely to remain so. In the current great political debate on Europe and Maastricht in the UK, federalism is often used as a term of abuse while subsidiarity is hailed as a mechanism through which the country will escape from the clammy clutches of the Brussels bureaucracy. However, away from these posturings, it has been pointed out that federalism can mean diversity rather than uniformity and subsidiarity is wholly consistent with decentralization and empowerment. Perhaps what is currently being created in the UK is a federalized administrative structure with no real powers and no political strategic direction. What it may require is a written constitution and a system of checks and balances to guide and protect its development. In brief, the scope for entrepreneurial behaviour or even basic administrative freedoms is held in check by central forces against which there is no appeal. This it might be argued is the reality of political administration — the centre controls and administrative structures comply. However, this is an old model of politics struggling to deal with a new model of management. If the latter is not protected then administrative innovation may rapidly loose its impetus and effectiveness.

UK GOVERNMENT PUBLICATIONS APPEARING IN
PARENTHETICAL REFERENCES IN THE TEXT:

Government Command Papers

Cm. 914, *The Financing and Accountability of Next Steps Agencies* (London: HMSO, 1989).

Cm. 1599, *The Citizen's Charter: Raising the Standard* (London: HMSO, 1991).

Cm. 1530, *Competing for Quality* (London: HMSO, 1991).

Cm. 1761, *The Government Reply to the 7th Report of the Treasury and Civil Service Committee* (London: HMSO, 1991).

Cm. 2101, *The Citizen's Charter: First Report* (London: HMSO, 1992).

Cm. 2111, *The Next Steps Agencies: Review 1992* (London: HMSO, 1992).

House of Commons Papers

HC. 348 (1988-9), House of Commons Treasury and Civil Service Committee, 5th Report, *Developments in the Next Steps Programme* (London: HMSO).

HC. 481 (1989-90), House of Commons Treasury and Civil Service Committee, 8th Report, *Progress in the Next Steps Initiative* (London: HMSO).

HC. 496 (1990-1), House of Commons Teasury and Civil Service Committee, 7th Report, *The Next Steps Initiative* (London: HMSO).

HC. 249 (1991-2), The National Audit Office, *The Vehicle Inspectorate: Progress as an Executive Agency* (London: HMSO).

HC. 390 (1992-3), House of Commons Treasury and Civil Service Committee, *The Civil Service* (London: HMSO); on-going inquiry.

HC. 390-i (1992-3), House of Commons Treasury and Civil Service Committee, *The Responsibilities and Work of the Office of Public Service and Science* (London: HMSO, January 1993).

HC. 390-ii (1992-3), House of Commons Treasury and Civil Service Committee, *The Civil Service,* evidence of Sir Robin Butler (London: HMSO, March 1993).

Other Government Publications

Efficiency Unit, *Improving the Management of Government: The Next Steps* (London: HMSO, 1988); also often known either as the Next Steps Report or the Ibbs Report).

Efficiency Unit, *Making the Most of Next Steps: The Management of Ministers' Departments and their Executive Agencies* (London: HMSO, 1991); also often known as the Fraser Report.

HM Treasury, *Policy Evaluation: A Guide for Managers* (London: HMSO, 1988).

HM Treasury, *Executive Agencies: A Guide to Setting Targets and Measuring Performance* (London: HM Treasury, 1992).

1.   Sir Robin Butler, "The New Public Management: The Contribution of Whitehall and Academia," *Public Policy and Administration,* Vol. 7, no. 3 (Winter 1993), pp. 1-14.

2.   Peter Hennessy, Evidence to the UK House of Commons Treasury and Civil Service Committee inquiry, *The Civil Service,* HC 390 (1992-3), May 4, 1993.

3.   A. Travis, "Shake Up for the Police the Biggest for Thirty Years," *The Guardian,* March 24, 1993.

4.   Norman Flynn, *Public Sector Management,* 2nd ed., (Brighton: Harvester Wheatsheaf, 1992); Christopher Hood, "A Public Management for All Seasons," *Public Administration,* Vol. 69, no. 1 (Spring 1991), pp. 3-19; Christopher Pollitt, *Managerialism and the Public Services* (Oxford: Blackwell, 1990).

5.   Sue Richards, "Changing Patterns of Legitimation in Public Management," *Public Policy and Administration,* Vol. 7, no. 3 (Winter 1993), pp. 15-28.

6.   For texts and articles dealing with these developments see: John Wanna, Cairan O'Faircheallaigh and Patrick Weller, *Public Sector Management in Australia* (Melbourne: Macmillan Australia, 1992); Jonathan Boston, "Assessing the Performance of Departmental Chief Executives: Perspectives from New Zealand," *Public Administration,* Vol. 70, no. 3 (Autumn 1992), pp. 405-28; Enid Wistricht, "Restructuring Government New Zealand Style," *Public Administration,* Vol. 70, no. 1 (Spring 1992), pp. 119-54; David Osbourne and Ted Gaebler, *Reinventing Government* (Reading Mass.: Addison-Wesley, 1991).

7.   Peter Hennessy, *Whitehall* (London: Secker and Warburg, 1989).

8.   See Colin Thain and Maurice Wright, "Planning and Controlling Public Expenditure in the UK: Part I, The Treasury's Public Expenditure Survey," *Public Administration,* Vol. 70, no. 1 (Spring 1992), pp. 3-24 and Part II, "The Effects and Effectiveness of the Survey," Public Administration, Vol. 70, no. 2 (Summer 1992), pp. 193-224.

9. Peter Hennessy, *Whitehall;* Les Metcalfe and Sue Richards, *Improving Public Management* (London: Sage, 1987).

10. Andrew Gray and Bill Jenkins with Andrew Flynn and Brian Rutherford, "The Management of Change in Whitehall: The Experience of the FMI," *Public Administration,* Vol. 69, no. 1 (Spring 1991), pp. 41-59.

11. UK Prime Minister's Efficiency Unit, *Improving the Management of Government: The Next Steps* (London: HMSO, 1988).

12. For an account of the genesis of the Next Steps report (often known as the Ibbs's report) see Peter Hessessy, *Whitehall,* pp. 619-22. Further see Andrew Flynn, Andrew Gray and Bill Jenkins, "Taking the Next Steps: The Changing Management of Government," *Parliamentary Affairs,* Vol. 43, no. 2 (April 1990), pp. 159-78.

13. Andrew Gray and Bill Jenkins, "Change in the Public Sector: Implementing the Next Steps," paper presented at seminar held by UK Public Administration Committee (PAC) and Civil Service College, May 1992.

14. Peter Kemp, "Can the Civil Service Manage by Contract?", *Public Money and Management,* Vol. 10, no. 3 (Autumn 1990), p. 31.

15. UK House of Commons Treasury and Civil Service Committee, 8th Report, *Progress in the Next Steps Initiative,* HC. 481 (1989-90) (London: HMSO), para. 1.

16. UK House of Commons Treasury and Civil Service Committee, 7th Report, *The Next Steps Initiative,* HC. 496 (1990-91) (London: HMSO), para. 3.

17. UK Prime Minister's Efficiency Unit, *Making the Most of Next Steps: The Management of Ministers' Departments and their Executive Agencies* (London: HMSO, 1991).

18. Cm. 1761, *Government Reply to the 7th Report of the Treasury and Civil Service Committee* (London: HMSO, 1991), p. 5.

19. Next Steps Unit, *Next Steps Briefing Note* (London: Next Steps Unit, April 1993) (mimeo), paras. 30-33.

20. Compulsory competitive tendering (CCT) and market testing require public sector organizations to put specifed sectors of their work out to tender. Regulations governing this process vary from area to area but in-house bids are generally permitted. As a consequence civil servants

or local government officers may be forced to bid to retain their own jobs or, if the tender goes elsewhere, be transferred to a private sector contractor. For examples of UK central government work currently exposed to market testing see Cm. 2101, *The Citizen's Charter: First Report* (London: HMSO, 1992), p. 59.

21.   Sir Robin Butler, evidence to Treasury and Civil Service Committee inquiry, *The Civil Service,* HC 390-ii, 1993, paras. 137-40.

22.   Andrew Gray and Bill Jenkins, "Change in the Public Sector."

23.   J.B. Quinn, *Strategies for Change: Logical Incrementalism* (Homewood, Ill.: Irwin, 1980).

24.   See A.Davies and J. Willman, *What Next?: Agencies, Departments and the Civil Service* (London: Institute of Public Policy Research, 1992), pp. 15-23.

25.   See, for example, G. Mather, *Responsibility, Accountability and Standards in Government,* paper presented as evidence to House of Commons Treasury and Civil Service Select Committee as part of their inquiry HC. 390 (1992-93), *The Civil Service* (London: HMSO).

26.   Patricia Greer, "The Next Steps Initiative: An Examination of Agency Framework Documents," *Public Administration,* Vol. 70, no. 1 (Spring 1992), pp. 89-98.

27.   Peter Kemp in evidence to UK Treasury and Civil Service Select Committee, 7th Report, *The Next Steps Initiative,* HC. 496 (1990-1), (London: HMSO), p. 106.

28.   Next Steps Unit, *Next Steps Briefing Note,* paras. 15-16.

29.   HM Treasury, *Executive Agencies: A Guide to Setting Targets and Measuring Performance* (London: HM Treasury, 1992).

30.   UK Prime Minister's Efficiency Unit, *Making the Most of Next Steps,* Appendix A.

31.   See the discussion in Cm. 914, *The Financing and Accountability of Next Steps Agencies* (London: HMSO, 1989).

32.   Next Steps Unit, *Next Steps Briefing Note,* paras. 25-6.

33.   Andrew Gray, Bill Jenkins and Bob Segsworth (eds), *Budgeting, Auditing and Evaluation: Functions and Integration in Seven Governments* (New Brunswick, NJ: Transaction Publishers, 1992).

34.   See, for example, N. Carter, "Learning to Measure Performance: The Use of Indicators in Organisations," *Public Administration,* Vol. 69, no.

1 (Spring 1991), pp. 85-102; Christopher Pollitt, "Bringing Consumers into Performance Measurement," *Policy and Politics,* Vol. 16, no. 2 (April 1988), pp. 77-87.

35. Colin Thain and Maurice Wright, "Planning and Controlling Public Expenditure in the UK," Parts I and II.

36. Richard Mottram, Next Steps Project Manager in Cm. 2111, *The Next Steps Agencies: Review 1992* (London: HMSO, 1992), p. 6.

37. House of Commons Treasury and Civil Service Committee, 7th Report, *The Next Steps Initiative,* HC. 496 (1990-1), Appendix 11, p. 133.

38. Grant Jordan, "The Next Steps Agencies: From Management by Command to Management by Contract," *Aberdeen Papers in Accountancy, Finance and Management,* No. W6, University of Aberdeen, 1992.

39. See, for example, G.K. Fry, *The Changing Civil Service* (London: George Allen and Unwin, 1985); Andrew Gray and Bill Jenkins, *Administrative Politics in British Government* (Brighton: Harvester Wheatsheaf, 1985); Peter Hennessy, *Whitehall.*

40. Andrew Flynn et al, "Taking the Next Steps: The Changing Management of Government."

41. First Division Association, evidence to Treasury and Civil Service Committee inquiry, *The Civil Service,* HC. 390 (1992-3), paras. 202-95.

42. Robin Hambleton, "Decentralisation and Democracy in Local Government," *Public Money and Management,* Vol. 12, no. 3 (July-September 1992), pp. 9-20.

43. Andrew Gray et al, "The Management of Change in Whitehall: The Experience of the FMI," p. 59.

44. See, for example, Sue Dopson, "Are Agencies an Act of Faith?", *Public Money and Management,* Vol. 13, no. 2 (April-June 1993), pp. 17-23; Elizabeth Mellon, "Executive Agencies: Leading Change from the Outside In," *Public Money and Management,* Vol. 13, no. 2 (April-June 1993), pp. 25-31.

45. Andrew Gray and Bill Jenkins, "Codes of Accountability in the New Public Sector," *Journal of Accounting, Auditing and Accountability* (forthcoming).

46. Sue Richards, "What After Next Steps?", working paper, (London: Public Management Foundation, 1993); David Walker, "Analysis: The Commanding Heights," radio program broadcast on BBC Radio 4, May 16, 1993.

47. Next Steps Team, *Next Steps Briefing Note 1993,* Annex D.

48. National Audit Office, *The Vehicle Inspectorate: Progress as an Executive Agency,* HC. 249 (London: HMSO, 1992), p. 5.

49. Peter Taylor-Gooby and Robin Lawson (eds), *Markets and Managers* (Buckingham: Open University Press, 1993).

50. See, for example, Bill Jenkins and Andrew Gray, "Evaluation and the Consumer: the UK Experience," chap. 26 in J. Mayne *et al.* (eds), *Advancing Public Policy Evaluation: Learning from International Experiences* (Amsterdam: North Holland, 1992); S. Miller and F. Peroni, "Social Policy and the Citizen's Charter," chap. 13 in N. Manning and R. Page (eds), *Social Policy Review 4* (Canterbury: Social Policy Association, 1992).

51. Christopher Pollitt, "Bringing Consumers into Performance Measurement."

52. Sir Peter Kemp, evidence to Treasury and Civil Service Select Committee inquiry, *The Civil Service,* May 4, 1993, paras. 368-77.

53.   Sue Richards, "Pity the Poor Bloodly Infantry," *Public Money and Management,* Vol. 13, no. 2 (April-June 1993), p. 6.

54. See, for example, A. Travis, "Equality Rules dropped in Sell-Off Push," *The Guardian,* May 24, 1993.

55. While the Department of Environment funded a critical evaluation of compulsory competative tendering in UK local government there seems to be no emprical basis to support "market testing" in central government on the scale proposed. Further see Sue Richards and Jeff Rodrigues, "Strategies for Management in the Civil Service: Change of Direction," *Public Money and Management,* Vol. 13, no. 2 (April-June 1993), pp. 33-8.

56. Sue Richards and Jeff Rodrigues, "Strategies for Management in the Civil Service," pp. 35-7.

57. See, for example, G. Mather, *Responsibility, Accountability and Standards in Government;* David Walker, "Analysis: The Commanding Heights."

58. Grant Jordan, "The Next Steps Agencies: From Management by

Command to Management by Contract," pp. 17-28.

59. HM Treasury, *Policy Evaluation: a Guide for Managers* (London: HMSO, 1988).

60. Sue Richards, "What After Next Steps?".

61. John Stewart, *Accountability to the Public* (London: European Policy Forum, 1992).

Appendix A

Next Steps Executive Agencies Established as of April 5, 1993

(Agencies indicated in **bold** were new as of April 5, 1993)

	STAFF[1]
Accounts Services Agency	85
ADAS Agency	2,280
Army Base Repair Agency	**3,800**
Building Research Establishment	700
Cadw (Welsh Historic Monuments)	245
Central Office of Information[2]	620
Central Science Laboratory	375
Central Statistical Office	1,235
Central Veterinary Laboratory	615
Chemical and Biological Defence Establishment	600
Chessington Computer Centre	**450**
Child Support Agency	3,500
Civil Service College	230
Companies House[2]	1,035
Compensation Agency[3]	150
Defence Analytical Services Agency	130
Defence Operational Analysis Centre	175
Defence Postal and Courier Services	485
Defence Research Agency[2]	11,260
Directorate General of Defence Accounts	2,460
Driver and Vehicle Licensing Agency	4,450
Driving and Vehicle Testing Agency[3]	260
Driving Standards Agency	1,900
Duke of York's Royal Military School	95
DVOIT	480
Employment Service	44,610
Fire Service College[2]	285
Forensic Science Service	615
Government Property Lawyers	**130**
Her Majesty's Prison Service	**37,420**

(Appendix A continued)

	Staff[1]
Historic Royal Palaces	350
Historic Scotland	630
Her Majesty's Stationery Office[2]	3,175
Hydrographic Office	815
Insolvency Service	1,530
Intervention Board	970
Laboratory of the Government Chemist	330
Land Registry[2]	9,510
Medicines Control Agency[2]	325
Meterological Office	2,460
Military Survey	1,155
National Physical Laboratory	790
National Weights and Measures Laboratory	50
Natural Resources Institute	440
Naval Aircraft Repair Organisation	1,630
National Engineering Laboratory	375
National Health Service Estates	140
National Health Service Pension Agency	630
Northern Ireland Child Support Agency[3]	700
Occupational Health Service	125
Ordnance Survey	2,280
Ordnance Survey of Northern Ireland[3]	210
Patent Office[2]	1,015
Paymaster General's Office	855
Pesticides Safety Directorate	170
Planning Inspectorate	605
Public Record Office	445
Queen Elizabeth II Conference Centre	60
Queen Victoria School	65
Radiocommunications Agency	535
RAF Maintenance	12,855
Rate Collection Agency[3]	280
Recruitment and Assessment Services Agency	190
Registrars of Scotland	1,295

(Appendix A continued)

	STAFF[1]
Royal Mint[2]	1,005
Royal Parks	260
Scottish Agricultural Science Agency	145
Scottish Fisheries Protection Agency	215
Scottish Office Pensions Agency	185
Scottish Prison Service	4,600
Scottish Record Office	125
Service Children's Schools Agency	1,110
Social Security Agency[3]	5,100
Social Security Benefits Agency	64,215
Social Security Contributions Agency	8,745
Social Security Information Technology Agency	4,090
Social Security Resettlement Agency	455
Teachers Pension Agency	290
The Buying Agency[2]	90
Training and Employment Agency[3]	1,670
Transport Research Laboratory	685
United Kingdom Passport Agency	1,290
Valuation and Lands Agency[3]	360
Valuation Office	5,030
Vehicle Certification Agency	75
Vehicle Inspectorate[2]	1,780
Veterinary Medicines Directorate	75
Warren Spring Laboratory	285
Wilton Park Conference Centre	25
89 agencies in number Total staff:	269,570
Less armed force personnel	7,730
Total civil servants	261,840
Customs and Excise[4] (30 executive units)	25,610
Inland Revenue[4] (34 executive offices)	63,105
Grand Total	350,555

SOURCE: "Next Steps: Briefing Note" (London: Cabinet Office, April 1, 1993).

1. October 1992 figures, excluding casuals, except new agencies which show staffing at launch date. Part-time staff are counted as half units.
2. Trading Fund status.
3. Part of Northern Ireland Civil Service.
4. Departments operating on "Next Steps" lines. Staffing for Inland Revenue excludes Valuation Office which is a free-standing agency.

Appendix B

Next Steps: Candidates for Agency Status as of April 5, 1993

	STAFF[1]
Army Logistics[2]	8,440
Defence Animal Centre	220
Defence Central Services	1,385
Directorate Information Technology Bureau	120
Driver and Vehicle Licensing (NI)[3]	150
Equipment Test and Evaluation	2,220
Fisheries Research Services	270
Fuel Suppliers Branch	20
Human Factors Research	390
Meat Hygiene Service[4]	1,800
Ministry of Defence Police	5,075
Naval Training and Recruitment	5,200
Office of Population Censuses and Surveys[5]	1,995
Property Holdings Portfolio Management	1,645
Royal Air Force Training	9,200
Surveyor General's Office	350
Transport and Security Services Division	1,235
War Pensions Directorate	1,250
Youth Treatment Service	200
19 agencies in number	Total: 41,165
Less armed services personnel	15,765
Total civil servants	25,400

SOURCE: "Next Steps: Briefing Note" (London: Cabinet Office, April 1, 1993).

1. October 1992 figures excluding casuals. Part-time staff counted as half units.
2. Estimated to require 8,440 staff drawn from a variety of sources.
3. Northern Ireland Civil Service.
4. Estimated to require 1,800 staff drawn from a variety of sources.
5. Independent government department. Responsible minister: Secretary of State for Health.

L O U I S   B E R N A R D

COMMENTS ON

BILL JENKINS' PRESENTATION

To those of us who are not fully familiar with the most recent developments on the British scene, the paper Bill Jenkins prepared with Andrew Gray provides a succinct yet complete description of the Next Steps initiative, useful references and, above all, a series of fundamental questions about the possible implications of such reform for our own political institutions.

I will limit my comments to three different aspects of the question: first, what caught my attention in the British experience; second, the situation here in Quebec with regard to government management reform; and third, the issues raised by the paper that could serve as a starting point for our discussion.

LESSONS FROM BRITAIN

The first thing that struck me in the Next Steps initiative is the very fact that it has been achieved. It has been done. It has become a *fait accompli,* since two out of three civil servants are already working for executive agencies rather than directly for departments or ministries. To my mind, this is a considerable feat.

This feat has been accomplished rapidly, in less than five years since

Margaret Thatcher's February 1988 statement. But let's not forget that preparations by the Efficiency Unit in the Cabinet Office took place during the previous decade. I take from this that you cannot launch such an initiative without first preparing the ground, conditioning people's minds and carefully charting your course. But I also conclude that once you're ready, you must act expeditiously. You do it, and let the chips fall where they may.

Another essential element for such a reform to succeed is the existence of a "champion team" with the ability to pilot the voyage around the many obstacles: "a dedicated band of change agents,"[1] as the paper puts it. It is interesting to note that on that team there were experienced managers from both the private and the public sectors. It was not purely an "in-house" affair.

An operation of that magnitude carried out over such a long period needs a "high level of political clout," but it also requires a great deal of political continuity and probably also a broad spectrum of agreement above party lines. What would have happened if the government led by John Major had not been re-elected in 1992? Would that have meant the end for the Next Steps initiative? This is an aspect that is not treated as such in the paper but that merits discussion.

THE QUEBEC SCENE

What is the situation here in Canada with respect to government management reform? I will restrict my comments to the Quebec scene, which I know better, and leave it to others to comment on the situation in other parts of Canada.

My own feeling is that, unfortunately, here in Quebec we are very far from making a deliberate and comprehensive attempt to reshape the management of government. The need is there, but the will is not. In the present Cabinet, there is overt opposition from some of the most senior ministers to any attempt to tamper with a strict application of the rule of absolute ministerial responsibility. Accountability of civil servants must remain exclusively to ministers who, alone, are responsible to the National Assembly and the public.

Of course, the government of the day pays lip service to the need for increased productivity in the delivery of public services and even goes as far as to refer to greater accountability from public managers as a means of achieving that goal. But, so far, no concrete gesture has been made in that direction. A delegation of senior civil servants recently went to London to study developments in the UK, but its favourable recommendations remained virtually unknown and unheeded.

It might be of historical interest to note that, some ten years ago, when I was Cabinet Secretary [in the Quebec government], I was instrumental in launching a pilot project whereby a minister was appointed to a new department called "Housing and Consumer Protection." The department essentially consisted of a regrouping of three or four administrative agencies, with the minister having virtually no direct administration duties but only policy responsibilities. My recollection of that experiment is that it proved to be no great failure, but no great success either. It did not survive the next cabinet reshuffle and did not create a precedent. This was an isolated attempt, and the time was not ripe.

Not much has been done since. In 1991, a bill was tabled in the National Assembly by a backbench government member which provided for the accountability of senior civil servants and heads of public bodies to the various standing committees of the Assembly. The Bill did not proceed, but it was reintroduced in 1993. It seems that, this time, conditions may be more auspicious. Let's hope this is the case.

ISSUES FOR DISCUSSION

I now turn to some of the main issues that Jenkins brought to our attention and which I hope we can discuss further.

The first is the political character of the reform. It seems that, in the UK, the originators of the reform have tended to downplay the political nature of their project, emphasizing managerial reform rather than political change. This may have been done for tactical reasons.

In order to avoid, or minimize, discussions of a political nature, the reformers have relied heavily on the assumption that administration and policy can be separated clearly. For, if this is so, administration can be entrusted to administrators and policy to politicians. Now, is it so? Jenkins seems to have doubts. "The good delivery of bad policy," he says, "is hardly the measure of a healthy state..."[2]

I, for one, strongly believe that delivery and policy are really two different things, and that it is useful to separate one from the other. If something goes wrong, for instance, it is of interest to know whether this comes from bad delivery, or from bad policy, or both. Methods to improve delivery and methods to change policies may be quite different. Managerial improvement will not cure political ailment; nor will political change get rid of administrative ineptitude.

On the other hand, managerial reform alone cannot achieve better government. In that sense, administration and policy are inseparable. Good government requires good delivery and good policy. But I venture to say that achieving good policy cannot be done through administrative reform but only through enhancement of the democratic process as such — through better political parties, stronger involvement by citizens, greater participation by voluntary organizations, an increased role for Parliament in policy evaluation, and more informed public discussion and reporting by the media. And this is where it becomes important to separate policy from delivery. In my opinion, we have a better chance of achieving good decision making by our elected representatives if their attention is centred on policy matters, rather than being distracted by administrative problems of all sorts. The political process can thus be more focussed on policy issues.

In this respect, one of the most interesting questions becomes how to organize not the executive agencies but the ministries themselves — the core — to enable the latter to perform adequately their role of policy making and implementation control. What kind of personnel do they need? What kind of background reports? What kind of intervention tools? To set up executive agencies is one thing, to restructure the core is another. Jenkins' paper hints that this important aspect of the British reform is less advanced than the implementation side.

Finally, I would like to suggest a short list of some of the important questions raised by Jenkins as they relate to our own institutions:

- Is the appointment of chief executives, sometimes from outside the civil service, and always on a contractual basis, compatible with our system of a career service?
- Will ministers be able to adapt to their new role and refrain from intervening in the daily business of the agencies?
- How will Parliament deal with the double responsibility or accountability of ministers and of chief executives?

- What will be the role of the Permanent Secretary of a ministry with respect to the chief executives of the agencies of that ministry? Could the former be by-passed through the direct access of chief executives to the Minister?

Any fundamental reform, of course, raises as many new questions as it answers old ones. It seems to me, however, that the Next Steps initiative has already accomplished a great deal and has laid the ground for further progress. One of its main objectives was "to change the culture of the civil service by making good management a valued and well rewarded activity."[3] This is worthy goal, and I sincerely hope it will be reached.

1. Bill Jenkins and Andrew Gray, "Reshaping the Management of Government: The Next Steps Initiative in the United Kingdom," in this volume, p. 80.
2. Jenkins and Gray, "Reshaping the Management of Government," p. 92.
3. Jenkins and Gray, "Reshaping the Management of Government," p. 75.

S U M M A R Y   O F   D I S C U S S I O N

Bill Jenkins was asked about the British Parliament's reaction to the creation of executive agencies in the United Kingdom. He responded that Parliament has welcomed not only the creation of agencies but also the opportunity to question agency chief executives. As he put it, Parliament wants to retain the ability to probe as deeply as possible. Overall, there has been little political opposition to reform. It is true, however, that the right would like to see more privatization and that Labour regards means-testing as threatening the civil service.

One participant asked what happens to the budget savings of an agency. Jenkins responded that those agencies with trading funds can carry over their surplus to the next fiscal year (presently, there are 12 agencies with trading funds and others can apply to become such). For those that are not, there are negotiations with the Treasury on a case by case basis. Jenkins added that, unless you can do what you say you will do in your objectives, what is the point of saving money?

Another participant drew on the British experience with the Next Steps initiative to make comparisons with Quebec. She said that, presently, government administrative reform in Quebec is focussed on the issue of public finance. The Treasury Board is receptive to any agency that can cut costs, but this bias is dangerous. The participant questioned how far we could go with a patchwork system for reform if we have not thought clearly about the concepts behind the reform.

A third participant reflected on the question of whether, in the British case, ministries will continue to be needed. Jenkins noted that while this might be a worthwhile question, *realpolitik* gets in the way of providing a concrete answer. He added, as an example, that pressures to appoint loyalists to government office may conflict with moves to reduce the number of ministries.

REINVENTING GOVERNMENT:

PRIORITIES AND POTENTIAL

One of the key tasks that all of us will have in the next few years is to educate ourselves, our staffs, our elected officials, our employees' unions, the media and our fellow citizens about the changes that are needed in government. We also have to educate ourselves and everyone else about *why* we need to change and how we can go about it. We have to establish the educational dialogue that will allow us to determine the values of the 1990s and the 2000s as the basis for governmental structure and functioning. To do this, we are going to need to be persuasive, and to have information, facts and figures, because some people respond to facts and figures. But we are also going to have to have a sense of values and be able to communicate those values — the new values — around which we are going to reinvent and reshape our governments.

In doing this, we are going to have to unlearn much of what we thought we knew, and relearn and be able to put together the kinds of things we'd like to put together in terms of our government structure and roles, and the interplay among the various segments of society. Moreover, we will need to blend the full resources of society.

Let me give you some numbers about government in the United States, so that we can understand what we are talking about. There are 83,462 governments in the US. One school district drops off about once a week, so the number keeps changing. Fifty years ago, there were 60,000 school districts; since then, we have consoidated these into 14,000. There is one federal government, and there are 50 state governments, 3,026 county governments, 19,000 municipal governments, 16,000 townships and 29,000 special districts.

There are 18.4 million Americans working for government on a full- or part-time basis. Three million of these work at the federal level; the rest, 15 million Americans, work at the state and local levels. One out of six employees works for government in the US. This is a huge industry, and Americans don't much care for government workers. They don't much like what they do or how they do it, by and large. As a result, the US has cut off the spigots, the sources of dollars. Americans are continuously shrinking the dollars they are willing to launder through government because they do not feel they are getting the "right kind of bang for the buck."

Here are some more figures to help illustrate this. As you know, Ronald Reagan hated government, and he said that many times. When he took office in 1980, debt service on the federal debt was US$52 billion per year. When he left office in 1989, the debt service was US$192 billion per year. According to predictions, the federal debt service is going to be US$770 billion at the turn of the century if the American people continue to loan the government money.

The number of dollars being drained from this economy is incredible. There is no other economy on earth that could have removed US$290 billion between 1980 to 1992 and still let committed government employees think that there would be discretionary income left to spend on anything they care about.

Another factor is the massive decline in middle-class family income since 1970. This has been partly masked by the fact that in 1970, only 46 percent of women between 25 and 65 were in the workforce on a full- or part-time basis, compared to 86 percent now. The reduction in middle-class income means that disposable, discretionary family income drops and people buy less. As a result, less sales tax is collected, and there is less income tax for funding local public services, including schools. In the next ten years, every government in the US is going to have fewer dollars, unless they are in a high growth area, and this reduction has nothing to do with recession. It has to do with the fact that the middle-class tax base is shrinking.

Now, the good news is that in about 2010, the shrinking will start to reverse itself, because we will have started to pay off the investment in technology and society. But for the next decade, in my opinion, government is not going to be allowed to have more dollars given to it. The American public is not willing, yet, to turn loose more money. Forty-two states have a clone of Proposition 13, which limits the amount of taxation on property. Proposition 13 alone has drained US$120 billion from California's governmental economy in the last 14 years. In addition, the indexing of income tax and the repeal of the inheritance tax and all the other things we have either voted for ourselves by ballot initiative or through the legislature, resulted in the loss of another US$80 billion to the governmental economy. This amounts to US$200 billion that public officials were able to rely upon 16 years ago that is no longer at their disposal.

Furthermore, there is no reason to believe that in the next 16 years the projected equivalent of US$200 billion will materialize for public sector spending. Moreover, five other states have even more draconian measures than Proposition 13 on the ballot this year to control public spending. The tax revolt is not dead by any means. So, if we believe governments are not going to have more dollars in the future, it is very important that government employees think through what options they are going to have. The Roosevelt Era mentality is over.

All societal groups, other than family/tribal societies, form governance structures to collectively solve problems. So government has been with us for as long as we know. No one gave government to us. We have constructed it ourselves, and have constantly changed it ourselves, over time. We have permission to change government.

Next we need to consider the ways that change in government has been attempted in the US in the past. First we started trying to change government at the federal level with appointment of the Hoover Commission, right after World War II. The Commission consisted of a coalition of business people, who were asked to use their business-oriented methods to improve government functioning. The net result, along with the results of the "little Hoover commissions" that sprang up in many states, cities and counties across the country, was to educate many business people about how different government is, and how difficult it is to manage in the public sector as opposed to the private sector.

Not much real change in government resulted from the Hoover

commissions. This was because we, as a society, do not want governments to be operated like businesses. We would just as soon not have our important public policy decisions made overnight, behind closed doors, solely on the basis of profit, by one person. We would just as soon have our public policy and service decisions made out in the open, and by more than one person, and to take a little bit longer so we can build a coalition, a broader based understanding and consensus. We would just as soon have profit perhaps as one of the criteria, but not the only criterion by which decisions are made.

A quote from Peter Drucker's book on innovation and entrepreneurship is valuable here:

> Public service institutions such as government agencies, labour unions, churches, universities, schools, hospitals, community and charitable organizations, need to be entrepreneurial and innovative fully as much as any business does. Indeed, they may need it more. Yet public service institutions find it far more difficult to innovate than even the most bureaucratic company. Governmental institutions are good at building empires; they always want to do more of the same; they resist abandoning anything they are doing; and they rarely innovate, once they have been established.[1]

Drucker gives three main reasons why governments do not innovate:

1) Public service institutions are financed on the basis of budgets rather than results. Success in a public institution is measured by getting a larger budget, rather than by attaining results.

2) Public service institutions depend upon a multitude of constituents. In a business that sells its products on a market, one constituent, the consumer, eventually overrides all of the others. The business needs only a very small share of a small market to be successful. Then it can satisfy other constituents, whether they be shareholders, workers, the community etc. But precisely because public service institutions have no results to determine their revenues, any constituent, no matter how marginal, has, in

122

effect, a veto power. Anybody can veto what we try to do. The moment a public service institution starts an activity, it acquires a constituency which then refuses to have the program abolished or even significantly modified. There are always people who hang on to any program that we start.

3) The most important reason for the existence of public service institutions, after all, is to do good. This means that they tend to see their mission as a moral absolute rather than an economic mission subject to a cost/benefit calculus. Economics always seeks a different allocation of the same resources to obtain a higher yield. In public service institutions, there is no such thing as a higher yield. If you are doing good, then there is no better. This means that public service institutions seek to maximize rather than to optimize. The closer a public service institution comes to attaining its objectives, the more frustrated it will be and the harder it will work on what it is already doing.[2]

So in other words, according to Drucker, decision makers in the private sector will often attain about 75 or 80 percent of a goal, but will then drop the goal because they realize that the dollars needed to get to 100 percent of the goal are so difficult to obtain that it is not worth pursuing the original plan. In contrast, in the public service arena, the closer we can get to solving homelessness, battered women's syndrome or any problem, the harder we work on accomplishing the original goal. More resources are put into the goal, not less, as goal achievement appears to be occurring. So, governments operate with a totally different psychology from that of the business community. This difference in psychology explains why the efforts of the Hoover commissions were not successful at changing governments. Business and government operate from very different premises.

Next we tried to change government by using the influence of academic institutions. We asked university professors to come in and study government, and see what they could do. As you know, not much has happened as a result of that. We even asked the League of Women Voters to come in and study the change process. While they are nice, pleasant people, they did not leave a long trail of lasting change in government.

We then tried to change government by using the "big six" consulting companies to change government. The idea behind conducting studies is that people make decisions based on logic. Unfortunately, this is not true. We don't make decisions based on logic; we make decisions in the private and public sectors based on our gut feelings and values, on power and politics, and on a lot of other things. As for the implementation of studies related to change, in the public sector one-third of studies are implemented and two-thirds sit on shelves. In the private sector, it is just the opposite: one-third sit on shelves and two-thirds are implemented. Two-thirds of studies are implemented in the private sector because of the impact on the bottom line. In government, two-thirds of studies are not implemented because when they were done, no one took into account that implementation would cause people to lose power or turf. So, studies are blocked or stopped cleverly, and spending money on "outside studies" in government has not resulted in much change.

Finally, politicians running as "outsiders" tried unsuccessfully to change government. When David Osborne and I travelled around the country for five years doing our research, we looked for places, at any level of government, where innovation was taking place. We did not care what the innovation was, but we wanted to know how it happened — what conditions had to exist for any kind of change to occur. Our research gave us great hope for the future of our society, for the future of public service and for the future of governance.

We concluded that the only successful way of changing government is to change it from the inside. This is the principle that excited David Osborne and me when we examined how things were changing in government. Government agencies were successful when they invested in their employees and helped them see how they could go about changing things from the inside.

The overwhelming conclusion of our book was that in government we have good people trapped in bad systems. The problem is, all our rules are written to go after that one percent to make the other 99 percent feel that they are stealing and are not to be trusted. So because of the way the rules are written for the one percent, the message gets to other employees that their creativity should be inhibited. We have constantly done this.

When I say "good people trapped in bad systems," I am talking about internal management systems of government: budget systems, civil service systems, personnel systems, procurement and purchasing systems, accounting systems, some of the revenue-generating systems, hierarchical organizational management systems, communication/information flow systems, agenda processes, the lack of strategic planning systems. Making changes does not generate sexy slogans at campaign time, and elections are not won or lost based on promises of changing these internal systems. As a politician or candidate running for public office, one would not proclaim, "Elect me, I'm going to change the procurement system!"

Mayors have come and gone; governors have come and gone; presidents have come and gone; school superintendents and officials have come and gone. But not a lot has changed, because there is not much incentive to make changes. By and large, investing in public employees, empowering them and helping them through changes, is something that can be done by changing the incentives for their current behaviour. This is the key.

The reason is that officials themselves know more about government, governance and the interplay among agencies, than the average citizen. Secondly, these forces affect them in some way or other. Thirdly, and most importantly, a number of officials have signed up to work for government because they have more than a little tug of altruism in them. I would just as soon have people who know more, who care about it, who are affected by the workings of government, and who are participating out of a sense of altruism, involved in bringing about change in government.

If the future has fewer governmental dollars in it, then government employees will make very different decisions as they think through their options. In the post-Roosevelt Era, we are going to have to be far more resourceful. Increasingly, agencies are going to have to learn to be more self-sufficient and fully utilize their full resources. This financial situation brings about a second role change for government officials. The first role change was to become educators. The second is to be marketers. Governments are going to have to market their services. This will have to be done in a very different way — principally in coalitions with other people. This is what is exciting. Because of the Roosevelt Era mentality, we have been relying on other people in government to do marketing. The question is how can we go about making coalitions for change at the local level, taking into account there will probably not be sufficient tax money available.

Now I want to talk about one of the ten principles of reinventing government. The first principle and the most astonishing is found in chapter one of our book: what we called "catalytic government." In the Roosevelt Era, we were service providers. But we are not going to be allowed to provide services in the future, because the American people are essentially cutting off the dollars for direct services provided by government. But government *can* play the catalytic role.

The original word of "government" in Greek means "to steer" not to row. During the Roosevelt Era, government got into a lot of rowing with some very high-priced public employees. Again, the American public thinks that government needs to do something other than steer. By being a catalyst for change and for the provision of services, government can make sure things happen to enable people to meet their quality-of-life service needs, without necessarily doing it with government employees.

All governmental budgeting systems in the US have a built-in incentive for public employees to spend money. Otherwise: a) you do not get to keep it in your department; b) you don't get as much money next year if you don't spend your allocations for this year, which is why 40 percent of all government spending takes place in the last quarter of every fiscal year; and c) if you don't spend what you were allocated, you asked for too much.

Under the current budgeting systems there is no incentive for departments to save money. Americans knows that, so the voting public is not going to give government more money until we clean up our act internally and change some of these systems. Developing ways to change the internal management systems of government is a pressing issue.

The challenge of a leaner future is to provide services without a lot of bureaucratic nonsense, without a lot of baggage dragging behind us, and to create a taxpaying clientele that likes what governments do and how they do it. Further, the challenge is to create a relationship with the taxpaying clientele in which they would want to form coalitions with government agencies, and not see government as a drag upon society that is sucking up tax dollars. We are going to have to rethink, and pull together, all of the resources of society, meld and merge and match in a way that has been unimaginable until today.

Think how exciting it must have been 220 years ago helping frame the Constitution of the United States, having the audacity to build a new concept of government. To think selectively and critically, and pick out from the rubble of what we know and build something brand new. That is the challenge, the wonderful opportunity before us — to pick very carefully those things from the rubble of the past, those bricks that we want to include in the new structure. We are not going to keep the old masonry, and we are certainly not going to keep the same form, but we are going to help shape it.

Notes

1. Peter Drucker, *Innovation and Entrepreneurship* (New York: Harper and Row, Publishers), p. 177.
2. Drucker, *Innovation and Entrepreneurship,* pp. 177-80.

Experiencing a Sea Change in the Democratic Potential of Regulation

---

L I O R A   S A L T E R

EXPERIENCING A SEA CHANGE

IN THE

DEMOCRATIC POTENTIAL OF REGULATION

Ask anyone today about democracy in government and the likely response is a discussion of referendums, polling and the reform of party politics, or else a diatribe on accountability. To the extent that regulation is mentioned, it is in the context of accountability, or rather the lack of it. Regulation is popularly seen to be burdensome, a soon-to-be-eliminated relic of the past, an anomaly in a properly democratic system and a good example of everything that has gone wrong about government.

Interestingly, this picture of regulation is likely to be proffered by those who, in the context of issues such as financial securities, environment and reproductive technologies, among others, advocate more rather than less regulation. Regulation has enormous staying power despite its current bad press. Even after a decade of deregulatory rhetoric and genuine regulatory reform, few if any agencies have been dismantled, and some new ones have been created.[1] Regulators themselves can be quite cynical about regulatory reform, suggesting that the result is not always smarter or more streamlined regulation, but simply fewer regulations on the books.[2] Clearing out the "deadwood" regulations, which are easily ignored in any case, demonstrates quick action to politicians clamouring for proof that the regulatory burden has been lightened.[3] Of course regulation has also changed in response to pressures for reform.[4] For example, the CRTC is quite a different agency today from what it was a decade ago inasmuch as it now applies its regulations with much more flexibility, and has eliminated a great many of them. Yet regulation persists because it responds to the demands of many different constituencies inside and outside government.[5] And because regulation persists, even if sometimes in modified form, it is incumbent upon those interested in democracy in government to include regulation in the discussion.

This paper will explore the democratic potential of regulation, especially in light of regulatory reform in the last decade. It will argue that, contrary to much current thinking, there is considerable scope for democracy in regulation, but that this democratic potential has been diminished in the last decade, primarily because questions about democracy and regulation have been neglected in recent regulatory reform initiatives. The argument is presented in two parts. In the first part, it is suggested that regulation should be understood as a form of governance. From this perspective, regulation includes co-management (joint participation in decision making between government and industry), direct democracy (direct public involvement in regulatory decision making), due process (legal rights associated with fairness and due process) and policy making (determination of broad public interest). Each of these aspect of governance embodies a democratic potential, but each also compromises democratic decision making in some important ways.

The argument is then made that the democratic potential in regulation could be enhanced if attempts were made to counterbalance the various aspects of governance in regulation as opposed to strengthening any one of them (for example, due process) at the expense of others (for example, co-management). In the second part of the paper, the focus shifts to an exploration of how regulation has changed in the past decade in response to regulatory reform initiatives. Using the theoretical model of regulatory governance developed in the first part of the paper, I argue that co-management and due process in regulation have been strengthened in the last decade at the expense of policy making and direct democracy. Consequently, the democratic potential of regulation has been weakened. This "sea change in regulation" need not have happened, it is suggested, if more attention had been paid to issues of democracy in conjunction with regulatory reform.

In the academic literature, the neglect of the relationship of regulation and democracy is striking.[6] To be sure, several years ago, regulation was systematically compared to other forms of governance in a series of studies illustrating the choices governments can make about the instruments of public policy and its implementation.[7] Compared to taxation or educational programs, regulation was described as coercive. Although it was not the objective of these studies to explore the complexities of "coercion," little account was taken of how coercion might be combined with other, more democratic aspects of regulation. Indeed, the most common definitions of regulation used today still stress its coercive nature.[8]

Those advocating an approach stressing choice of governing instruments also suggested participation was beneficial. But to the extent that the issue of democracy was raised in their work, it was mainly in the context of a broader debate at the time about the accountability of regulation.[9] The consensus was then, and remains today, that regulation is not very accountable because regulators are appointed, not elected, and because they cannot easily be held accountable to a democratic system premised on ministerial responsibility, party politics and elections. Regulation is undemocratic by its nature, in other words, because of its weak links to a democratic process conceived of as representative democracy.

Ironically, at the same time the debate about accountability in regulation was occurring, significant measures were being undertaken to increase public participation in regulation.[10] Open hearings, as well as public meetings dealing with a broad span of policy issues, were experimented with and sometimes formally introduced as procedural innovations, especially but not only in environmental regulation.[11] In the academic literature, it was also argued that costs should be awarded to public interveners to permit them to participate on a more or less equal basis with industry.[12] A few agencies instituted procedures to award costs. It was further argued that regulation represented a new and important dimension of accountability.[13] Due process provisions were attached to environmental and other regulation, in an attempt to ensure fairness among the inevitable winners and losers created by regulatory decisions.[14] On the basis of this material, it could easily have been concluded that regulation offered one of society's few opportunities for direct democracy, i.e., for direct involvement, usually through public hearings, of the lay public in decision making on issues of immediate concern to them. Indeed an argument could be made that regulation was more democratic than the ordinary functions of government because it allowed for continued exchange of ideas between decision makers and their many publics.

No one has ever suggested that regulation is the perfect instrument for direct or any other type of democracy. Its propensity to capture and bureaucratic inertia, combined with its uncomfortable fit with the institutions of representative democracy, are too easily demonstrated.[15] If regulation is to be considered as a democratic instrument of governance, it is obviously a flawed instrument, fraught with contradictions.[16] But as recent public debates so amply illustrate, other instruments of governance are equally flawed.[17] As such, it is incumbent upon those concerned with democracy in government to include regulation in the discussion because of its democratic potential as well as its democratic deficiencies.

The argument that regulation embodies a democratic potential is based on theoretical analysis of the various aspects of regulation as a form of governance. The real test of the democratic potential in regulation is a practical one. To what extent are current perceptions of regulation as inherently undemocratic borne out by a detailed examination of regulatory practice? However important this question, it is very difficult to answer. Regulatory regimes differ so much from each other that generalizations are difficult to sustain, even assuming the analyst could command detailed knowledge about many regulatory regimes. The CRTC and environmental regulation are often used as the points of reference, but they bear little resemblance to the regulatory regimes that deal with the labelling of food additives or with highway safety.[18]

To move the discussion to a more practical level, it will be useful to focus on the debate about regulatory reform rather than on specific instances of regulation. Four keywords will be examined in section three of this paper: "consultation," "stakeholders," "risk" and "regulatory review." What does their frequent use today suggest about the practical orientation of regulation and its potential for democracy? In the concluding section of this paper, the democratic potential of regulation will be placed in the context of current debates about regulatory reform and deregulation. The paper is based on detailed research on broadcasting, telecommunications, environmental and pesticide regulations, and a recent study of regulation and competitiveness in which several regulatory reviews were examined.[19] The concept of keywords and the methodology used for their analysis in the second section are derived from Raymond Williams' *Keywords*.[20]

THE DEMOCRATIC POTENTIAL OF REGULATION

To the extent that regulation and democracy are linked in the academic literature, it is usually a negative association. Regulators are too easily captured by the more powerful of their constituents, it is argued, and regulators are not accountable. There is much evidence to support the negative view, but it is also contradicted daily by the efforts of regulators to incorporate their constituent publics into decision making and by procedural innovations designed to elicit participation. The challenge is to describe the democratic potential of regulation without discounting the well-documented problems.

Speaking positively first, it can be argued that the democratic potential of regulation lies with four facets of its operation. Regulatory regimes regularly (although not always) offer a venue for debate on issues before a decision is made, often in the form of public hearings which anyone may attend.[21] As well, hearings are required to be demonstrably fair to their participants.[22] In addition, regulators usually have the capacity to examine issues of immediate and pressing public concern. Finally, regulators function most effectively when they have established a relationship of reciprocity with the regulated industry.[23] In very different ways, each of these facets of regulation embodies a potential for democracy. But no one will be surprised if, on closer examination, this potential is quite often compromised or undermined, as happens, for example, when due process in public hearings results in court-like proceedings of benefit mainly only to lawyers. Both sides of the story must be canvassed if regulation is to be understood as a form of governance.

Regulation as an Example of Direct or Participatory Democracy

The easiest argument to make about the democratic potential of regulation is based on the public hearing process.[24] Open hearings provide the public with the opportunity to become directly involved with decision making. When they deal with both broad policy matters and specific decisions, hearings encourage public debate. When the definition of "interested parties" is broad enough to include those with a point of view, not just those with legal or financial interests, this public debate is unfettered.[25] It is likely to be more comprehensive than is possible even in an election campaign. When the regulator takes responsibility for the costs of intervention, the imbalance of resources among interveners is also addressed, and it becomes reasonable to expect that public contributions will be informed, if not expert.

Finally, to the extent that regulators demonstrate to their interveners that their views have been taken into account, members of the public receive more feedback from the regulatory process than they normally encounter elsewhere in politics. Of course, not all regulatory regimes incorporate public hearings, rely upon a wide definition of "interested parties" or make cost awards to public interveners. Moreover, many agencies take considerable pains to avoid broadening the issues under consideration or incorporating public debate and controversy. But these are relatively straightforward matters, which could, in theory at least, be resolved in favour of broadening the democratic potential of regulation with some additional modest reforms.

Two problems confounding the potential for direct public involvement in regulatory decision making are much more serious. The first problem concerns the public who are subject to being co-opted or made "professional" by virtue of their participation. Regulatory hearings are usually lengthy. Over time, as many commentators have noted, they socialize their participants to a common definition of the issues and problems to be solved. Legally or financially interested parties are not likely to lose sight of their goals; indeed the danger lies in the converse, when the interested parties redirect the attention of the regulator away from the legislated mandate to focus on the problems of the regulated industry exclusively. Those without legal or financial interests are less directly accountable and consequently more easily influenced by the unfolding debate over the course of time.

To protect themselves against co-optation, public participants often stake out a position concerning the social values implicated in any decision.[26] But because regulation necessarily involves compromise among competing views and interests, because social values are so notably impervious to compromise and because the regulator is likely to avoid controversies about social values, the result is that the public participants become isolated from the process. Seeking to protect themselves against potential co-optation, they alienate themselves from routine decision making and compromise. An alternative to alienation is to become "professional." Long-standing advocate groups ensure that their participants are held accountable, but, in this case, accountability is to the advocate group rather than to a wider public. Professional skills that accompany advocate group affiliation are also useful in avoiding co-optation. They aid advocate groups in handling the detailed and often highly complex issues that come before the regulator and ensure that such groups are capable of engaging productively in the negotiations that characterize all regulation. But professional skills also come at a price, not the least of which is the need to raise funds to support professional or expert participation. Considerable efforts of advocate groups are spent ensuring that they can participate at all, with the result that the democratic potential of direct democracy in regulation is compromised.

The second problem lies with regulators. In spite of significant efforts to encourage participation, their expectations of the public are decidedly unclear. In theory, regulators might use the hearings to benefit from a discussion of the social values underlying their decisions, as is certainly the case in rule making.[27] Alternatively, they might view the individual public participant as a repository of experience directly applicable to the decision at hand. In such case, the individual might contribute information about the effects of past decisions or about local conditions that need to be taken into account if regulation is to be successfully implemented. Alternatively, the public participant might be regarded as a survey sample, admittedly a very small sample, reflecting public opinion. Then again, the hearing might be regarded as a proper location for a public debate somewhat like a public meeting in an election campaign, or the regulator might consider the scientific and/or technical issues to be controversial, requiring debate among experts hired by those with conflicting interests. Finally, participation might well be regarded as a value in its own right, quite independent of any effect it might have on decisions.

In practice, few regulators have really decided what they want to achieve through public participation. Having not decided what expectations of participation are reasonable and appropriate in their specific case, they fail to set clear guidelines to encourage it. For example, when regional hearings are used as a sample of public opinion and only a few people show up, or when industry uses regional hearings as just another way of influencing the regulators, then benefits from regional hearings are discounted. Or when regulators travel to local communities but have not made their expectations known or asked community members to address specific questions on which only local residents have expertise, regulators hear the same refrain in the local communities that they hear elsewhere. The benefits from local hearings are wasted as a result. These and other attempts to encourage direct public involvement in decision making fail when regulators are themselves confused about what they want to achieve from direct democracy. The initiatives taken to encourage participation often undermine the democratic potential of regulation by promoting confusion, lack of feedback or a view of the public as irrelevant and quarrelsome.

Regulation as Delegated Legislation

Regulation is often described as delegated legislation. But it need not involve formal delegation in order to be legislative in orientation.[28] Regulation was originally conceived as a solution to the problems that legislators faced because of the highly technical nature of many decisions, the detailed, repetitive and occasionally routine nature of legislative action, and the need to connect policy with its detailed implementation.[29] As delegated legislators, in either the formal or informal sense of the term, regulators were expected to develop an appreciation of a specific sector or issue, and to use their accumulated expertise, along with other expert advice, to develop something akin to public policy, explicitly or through their case-by-case decisions. Like the legislatures that they are intended to complement, properly functioning regulatory agencies are supposed to be highly responsive to a wide variety of concerns, issues and problems.[30] This aspect of regulation also embodies a democratic potential. To the extent that regulators are adequately attuned to their many constituencies and responsive to their needs, they function as proxies for their elected counterparts. Indeed, regulators are often in a position to be more responsive than elected officials because they have intimate knowledge of the issues and problems in their areas of jurisdiction.

Two objections are raised to the notion that regulators are the formal or informal delegates of legislators — the problems of accountability and capture. Although both objections have merit, they are often overstated. In the case of accountability, it should be emphasized that regulators are not free to act as they choose, but must operate within a framework of their mandating legislation, either in general or quite specifically in the case of some regulators. Moreover, if the functions now assigned to regulators were to be rerouted back through the legislative process, departmental officials, also unelected and usually operating behind closed doors, would carry out many of the detailed tasks now performed by regulators. Add to this picture the fact that many regulatory agencies hold hearings, while departments normally do not. Furthermore, many regulatory decisions are simply recommendations to elected officials or are subject to the scrutiny and review of elected officials. The result is that regulation is probably no less accountable than what might reasonably replace it, perhaps more so.

In the case of capture, again regulators are no different from government departments, which are also subject to the type of influence derived from long and close associations. Departmental officials are further compromised by the need to promote economic well being in the sectors they deal with regularly.

In fact, what makes regulation interesting as a form of governance, and illustrates its democratic potential most clearly, is its close association with the community and the issues of its immediate concern. Regulation is, by nature, reactive. Regulators are highly dependent upon their many constituents to initiate proposals, to respond to the regulations, to identify problems worthy of attention and to examine the trade-offs inevitably involved when one course of action is chosen over another. In this sense, it is appropriate to consider regulation as a "bottom up" form of governance. The democratic potential of "bottom up" governance is obvious.

Equally obvious are the factors that might compromise the democratic potential of regulation as "bottom up" governance. To the extent that regulation reflects an unequal structure of representation, it is neither particularly open nor responsive.[31] When the influence of some participants exceeds that of others, and regulation becomes unduly responsive to some issues but blind to others, there is little democracy in regulation.[38] Most important, when the legislative mandate or the predilections of the regulator preclude consideration of a wide range of issues within the sector(s) being regulated, then the democratic potential of regulation, which is bound up with its "bottom up" character, is compromised. In this last case, the regulator fails to make proper use of its knowledge about the sector or issue being regulated because limitations, or self-limitations, have been imposed.

Regulation as Co-management

I have argued at some length elsewhere that regulation embodies co-management of the sectors being regulated.[32] This argument rests on the premise that regulators, regardless of how pro-active they are, must respond to the initiatives of those within the sector. In turn, this argument rests on the observations that regulators are dependent upon the industry to generate proposals or applications to which they can respond, that no regulatory initiative is undertaken without extensive consultation, that the enforcement of regulations required co-operation from the regulated industry, and finally that the public interest objectives of regulation cannot be achieved unless the regulator also promotes the health and profitability of the industries being regulated. The argument does not undermine the claim that regulation might be, by nature, coercive and interventionist. It is self-evident that, without regulation, industry is freer to act as markets dictate, even if industry often supports or initiates regulation. The point is also not whether regulation constitutes intervention or imposes burdens. On the contrary, even within a framework of intervention (or coercion), there is considerable room for mutual influence and reciprocity. At the very least, once it has been decided that regulation will apply, the relationship between the regulator and the regulated industries is, and must be, a two-way street.

The term "co-management" is new when applied to regulation. It is chosen to emphasize the two sides of regulation. On one side, by regulating industry, government assumes some powers normally associated with its management. It imposes objectives upon industry that otherwise would be absent. But the other side of regulation is also important. Industry is always involved in shaping the regulatory regimes to which it is subject, both initially when the regimes are being established, and in the routine exercise of regulation and rule making. "Co-management" draws attention to the reciprocity of the regulatory process, the obligations placed on both parties and the compromises always involved when those with different interests and perspectives are forced to work together in a continuing relationship.

Where is the democratic potential in co-management? To many people, co-management looks far too much like capture to be associated with democratic administration at all. This view is short-sighted. Co-management offers democratic potential inasmuch as the framework of intervention is one developed and imposed by elected legislators and inasmuch as the public interest is the purpose of the exercise. In other words, co-management can be more or less democratic depending upon the circumstances. Furthermore, by setting in place a regime of co-management, legislators open up the possibility that not just the industry will be involved in decision making. Once empowered, regulators must be seen to be responsive to many different constituencies, not just industry. Regulatory actions are themselves often subject to review. Finally, as regulated industries often discover to their dismay, their viewpoints do not always prevail in the decisions made by the regulator.

To suggest that co-management offers democratic potential is not to underestimate the shortcomings of co-management. The problems of regulatory capture are significant. Much of the literature on consultation assumes that it is only industry which needs to be consulted.[33] Moreover, to the extent that regulators only implement and enforce rules, but do not engage in rule making or grant permits and licences (where they have considerable discretion to co-manage), it makes little sense to characterize regulation as reciprocity and compromise. When regulators apply rules that they do not design, and when they lack discretion in enforcing rules, as is the case in some areas of regulation, the situation cannot be described as co-management. Whatever democratic potential rests in co-management is compromised as a result, and regulation becomes primarily coercive in intent and operation.

Democracy as Due Process

Regulation is often described in terms of its hybrid functions. These functions draw attention to regulation as delegated legislation, as we have done, and to its managerial character. Among the hybrid functions of regulation is that of adjudicating disputes. Indeed, some regulatory bodies are properly described as quasi-judicial, similar in their orientation and function to the courts. Even when regulators are not mainly quasi-judicial, however, regulatory decisions create winners and losers. An arbitration of interests is always involved even in matters of broad public concern. For example, when the CRTC recently considered the future of broadcasting at lengthy public hearings in which no application was pending, no one doubted that any resulting "policy" would benefit some current and potential licensees more than others by making it easier or more profitable for them to carry out their business.

To deal with the pressures of being adjudicative, some regulators have introduced court-like provisions in their procedures.[34] Agencies might permit cross-examination, for example, or full disclosure of information to the parties, Participants are often permitted to be represented by counsel. Public participants are accorded the formal status of "parties" to the dispute, even if no legal or financial interests are directly at stake. Regulatory bodies are not normally courts, of course. In the case of regulation, the standard is fairness. Regulators retain considerable discretion about how fairness is to be achieved, but some regulators institute as many court-like provisions as is possible, drawing comfort from legal norms of fairness and natural justice.

Fairness and natural justice are intimately bound up in currently held notions about democracy. Indeed, since the introduction of the Charter, some have argued that legal norms have replaced social values as the standard to be achieved in democratic administration. The point in this paper is not to join the debates about the effect of the "charterization" of public policy and the replacement of social with legal norms in public policy. Suffice to say that, to a greater or lesser extent, one conception of democracy is bound up with legal norms. Its application in regulation is increasingly commonplace.

Like other aspects of governance with democratic potential, due process is fraught with contradictions. Too often it becomes adversarialism, or what Arthurs calls "rampant proceduralism,"[35] i.e., debates between lawyers representing different interests and focussed mainly on rights (and wrongs) of participation. The substance of the issues is obscured, and the possibilities that participants will shape a final decision is undermined when all effort is focussed on winning legal and/or procedural issues. Moreover, because many regulators lack power to make final decisions and only issue recommendations, it is entirely possible that legal victories in the hearings will be followed by a substantive loss in the final decision. Both the elected legislators and the regulators, either of whom might make the final decision, must be fair, but they need not accept the substantive arguments of the parties, as those whose efforts are primarily oriented to principles of fairness often also find to their dismay.

Participants are usually well aware of the danger of relying upon procedural democracy to achieve substantive objectives. Less obvious are other costs of adversarialism. In replacing social values with legal norms, the regulator transforms the discourse of regulation and the status of par-

142

ticipants, thus undermining the democratic potential of regulation. Recall that one aspect of the democratic potential was bound up with the responsiveness of the regulator to viewpoints other than the regulated industry. Applying legal norms to regulation might well ensure that all participants have access to the open forums where decisions are being considered, but it cannot guarantee access to the actual assessments of the regulator. These often take place behind closed doors, sometimes because the open public hearings have become so adversarial. Seeing no hope of compromise, dismayed by the lengthiness of the proceedings and angered by the procedural — as opposed to substantive — nature of the hearings debate, regulators seek other venues for substantive decision making.

Moreover, legal norms are posited on the notion that all parties have financial or similar interests at stake, interests that must be protected through due process and natural justice. To be sure, some public participants do have interests, in the legal sense of the term, or at least something roughly equivalent to them. But others represent no large or easily identifiable constituency, nor anyone with something specific to "win" or "lose." These last interveners reflect a viewpoint, not an interest. Their involvement in regulatory hearings is only intended to further their viewpoints through the public debate engendered in (and often only available through) the public hearing process. To them, regulation is interesting because of its policy-making function. When they enter a process whose primary orientation has become an adjudication of interests, however, they are treated as if they were interested parties. Integrated in a discourse shaped by legal norms, they have little alternative but to reshape their own discourse so that they too can be described as having an "interest." To the extent that they do, or that they fail to achieve effective participation (in spite of the rights achieved through the imposition of legal norms) because their "interest" is so diffuse, democracy is compromised. The public debate represented in and through regulation, which necessarily involves an exchange of viewpoints, becomes instead a debate among interested parties where those without identifiable interests are severely disadvantaged.

Democracy as Countervailing Forces

A case can be made that democratic regulation is an oxymoron. Truly, if regulation is compared to some ideal model of the democratic process, it cannot be said to be very democratic. But the point was made earlier that no instrument of governance is always and completely democratic. Legislators are undemocratic, for example, by virtue of the fact that they are elected infrequently and are seldom accountable for the detailed decisions they make. Government departments derive their democratic accountability from their ministers' responsibility, but their daily practices conform to few expectations of democracy, even when consultation becomes routine. Polling and referendums are now in vogue, but their democratic potential is compromised by the fact that they are sporadic, that they deal with broad policies and that they often reflect only the fleeting pre-occupations of the notoriously fickle public. Tripartite councils easily become disconnected from those whose interests they represent. Neither collective bargaining nor self-regulation offers a panacea for those seeking democracy in government, nor do they constitute viable solutions for those entrusted with responsibility for the routine and detailed matters of governance. If regulation is flawed as a form of democratic administration, so too are all the other options.

Much more productive, especially given the staying power of regulation, is to examine regulation as a form of governance to see how its democratic potential can be strengthened and its deficiencies corrected. One answer, which has general applicability to all regulation, is to be found by using more than one approach to regulation, counterbalancing co-management with direct democracy, due process and policy making. For example, the tendency for co-management to shade into capture might be offset by the direct involvement of the public in public hearings on the same issues. Through the hearings, the regulatory process would be opened up in a manner that precludes capture. A regulatory agency that sought to balance the two would include open public hearings but also adequate means for consultation with its regulatory constituents and devolution of responsibility for some aspects of regulation to those same constituents. Such an initiative was taken when the CRTC wanted to respond to the problem of sex role stereotyping in broadcasting. It instituted a committee of interested parties to develop a plan for self-regulation, but it also debated the issue in open hearings and it also held to account broadcast licensees for their adherence to the self-regulatory codes through an open public hearing process. Similarly, while the interested parties in environmental regulation can resolve their disputes through an informal negotiation (i.e. co-management), some open vetting of their final decisions also needs to occur.

The tendency for direct democracy to be compromised when public advocates retreat into merely articulating their social values, or when regulators fail to use participation effectively, might be offset by considering the task to be done in regulation as co-management, and by devolving significant responsibilities to the participants. Once involved in co-management, participants would be integrated fully into routine but important functions of governance. Of course this second suggestion would also require expanding the notion of co-management to include more than the regulator and industry among the participants in regulation. In the previous example, reliance upon self-regulation in broadcasting only contributed to the democratic potential of regulation because, in this instance, more than industry was involved in developing and implementing self-regulation.

Ensuring that public hearings remain a venue for direct involvement of the public in decision making would also counter the tendencies in regulation to rely upon legal norms that reshape public debate as legal discourse. Hearings that become loaded down with court-like procedures and legal wrangling do not further the democratic potential of regulation, notwithstanding the greater emphasis on due process that results. In turn, introducing the fairness provisions associated with legal norms and due process might offset the tendency of co-management to evolve into mere bargaining or interest group negotiations, or even capture. Far too often, in the current case of regulatory co-management, decisions appear to benefit one party or another, and, consequently, they appear to be unfair. Finally, conceiving their mandate broadly and themselves as proxies for legislators, regulators might remain more responsive to the problems and concerns of their many constituents. Far too often, today, regulators believe they are simply in the middle of an interest group negotiation, when matters of broad public policy should be discussed.[36]

There are many benefits from viewing the democratic potential in regulation as requiring a variety of different approaches, ranging from due process to co-management, from direct public involvement to policy making. Most obvious is the possibility that the negative effects of any single approach will be offset by the more complex process. Using different approaches in combination with each other also ensures that each of the various groups affected by regulation has its say in a context that encourages its type of participation. Furthermore, simply by paying attention to balancing the various approaches, regulators are more likely to become aware of what they are doing and, more importantly, why they are doing it. No longer are they likely to engage in public hearings only to be disappointed because they, the regulators, have failed to specify in advance what they want to achieve from the hearings.

Attention to achieving an appropriately balanced approach in order to strengthen the democratic potential of regulation is likely to reduce costs and increase satisfaction with regulation in the longer term. Of course this balance among the various approaches will be different for each type of regulation. Environmental regulation, where open public hearings might well be stressed, will be different from telecommunications regulation, where a legal discourse will still prevail. The law, the type of decisions to be made and possible participants are different in each case.

THE REAL WORLD OF REGULATION

Needless to say, regulatory regimes differ significantly from each other. For example, although both are mandated by legislation, no one would confuse the CRTC with the Motor Vehicle Safety Inspection Branch or find they had much in common. Moreover, regulatory agencies change dramatically over their tenure. What might have been true about pesticide regulation, the AECB or the CRTC a decade ago might well no longer be true today: how, then, to explore the democratic potential in regulation in a practical way?

In *Keywords,* Raymond Williams argues that particular words function as signposts reflecting the prevailing orientations of the political process. Keywords set the terms of reference for public debate; they constitute "consensus." Keywords offer a reflection of what is normally taken for granted about social relations; consequently, they orient members of the community to public issues. Public policies follow. Williams suggests also that keywords change over time. By studying changes in terminology, he argues, one can also explore changes in the prevailing public discourse and policies. It is easy to identify the keywords in the regulatory debate and, moreover, to document how they have changed over the last two decades. Doing so might well prove beneficial in capturing the broad span of regulation, thereby indicating how approaches to regulation have changed. For the purposes of this paper, what is important is not the keyword itself, but its implications for the democratic potential of regulation. Four keywords have been selected as reflecting the regulatory debate: "consultation," "risk assessment," "stakeholders" and "regulatory reviews." These keywords apply across the wide span of regulatory regimes.

Consultation

On first impression, "consultation" is a synonym for participation and also implicitly for direct democracy. All three suggest that regulatory decisions should be shaped by dialogue with the public. Moreover, whatever the legal requirements for consultation (they are increasing, but consultation is only sometimes required by law), consultation has become the norm in regulation. To be sure, this consultation has often been interpreted as dialogue only with the regulated industry. Indeed, some commentators still decry the lack of consultation by regulators with industry, while others argue that agencies are captured by industry through the consultation process. Notwithstanding these concerns, participation is increasing. Yet even if industry were to be satisfied with the level of consultation and even if members of the public were included in the consultations, it would be mistaken to conflate consultation and direct democracy.

In order for high levels of public involvement in decision making to exist, two criteria must be met. First, there must be a devolution of responsibility for decision making to forums where participation actually occurs. This can happen in several ways. It can involve devolution of responsibility to a multi-party body reflecting the many interests and viewpoints of the regulator, industry, client and public groups, as was the case with the CRTC's initiatives on sex role stereotyping in broadcasting. It can involve establishing councils, made up of worker and/or client groups with a direct interest in the decisions to be made. Or it can simply involve investing public hearings with significant authority so that decisions clearly reflect discussions occurring there. These are all attempts to meet what might be called the institutional requirements for direct democracy. A second criteria is that every possible effort must be made to allow all those implicated in or affected by the decision meaningful roles within the decision making process. This is what might be called the participation requirement for direct democracy.

If these two criteria are applied to consultation, it becomes evident that consultation and direct democracy are very different. In consultation, institutional devolution of responsibility does not take place regardless of the degree of influence exerted by those consulted. Final decisions remain vested with the regulator, who in many cases also decides whom to include in the consultations and how such consultation will take place. Furthermore, nothing guarantees that all those implicated in the decision will even be consulted, let alone assigned a meaningful role. Consequently, even if wide-ranging consultations take place, direct democracy need not occur. The participatory requirement for direct democracy is also not met.

Stepping back from the issue of direct democracy, we should ask: what is the relationship of consultation to the democratic potential of other aspects of regulation — namely, due process, delegated legislation and co-management? Because consultation is usually quite informal, due process provisions, and the legal norms accompanying them, have little role to play. Consultation does render regulation highly responsive to the needs and concerns of its many constituents. But the increasing emphasis on consultation has been accompanied by a significant reduction in the scope of regulation and the discretion of regulators, especially with respect to their policy making functions.

Thus, while consultation does increase the capacity of regulators to be intimately involved with the issue or sector being regulated, the democratic potential embodied in regulation as delegated legislation is curtailed because regulators are not permitted to be "proxy legislators." They do not have the scope of action or degree of discretion normally attributed to legislators. In fact, today, it might be fair to characterize much regulation as being simply a conduit between elected legislators on one hand and those affected by legislation and rules on the other. Similarly, while consultation appears to strengthen the co-management aspect of regulation, the scope of co-management has also been decreased. Many limitations have been placed upon regulators to respond to problems and concerns within their sector. Highly consultative regulators co-manage more, it seems, but in today's deregulatory climate, they often co-manage about fewer issues.

Stakeholders

The term "stakeholder" is often used today to refer to all participants in regulation. It is premised on two related arguments. The first is that all participants, even those expressing a viewpoint, have an interest in regulatory decisions. In this case, public participation is equated with the "not in my backyard" syndrome. Participant interests arise from the economic benefits or losses created through regulation because regulation creates winners or losers, or because regulation imposes a "tax," or because it is redistributive in orientation. Participant interests also arise from the organizational or status "rewards" that all participants — including regulators — potentially collect by virtue of their involvement. It is assumed, in other words, that no one will participate in regulation unless it is in their interests to do so, and that participation in debates about important public issues has no value in its own right.

The second argument builds upon the first. It is that regulation is best conceived of as an interest group negotiation and as forum for bargaining among interested parties. In this case, anything which might improve the prospects for efficient bargaining and successful negotiations of interests is to be encouraged. Regulators are currently experimenting with stakeholder mediation, for example, where likely participants, conceived of as stakeholders, are engaged in a variety of bargaining strategies designed to achieve a successful outcome for as many of them as possible.

How does the democratic potential of regulation associated with co-management, direct democracy, due process and delegated legislation fare when participants are viewed as stakeholders? Some have suggested that the democratic potential is realized by innovations such as stakeholder mediation. Certainly the co-management aspects of regulation are enhanced. Moreover, to the extent that many publics are included among the stakeholders, even the direct democracy aspects of regulation can be strengthened by a stakeholder approach. At the same time, several points should be noted about the association of stakeholders with the notion of democracy in regulation. First, it is quite likely that those with a diffuse interest will not be able to represent themselves effectively as stakeholders. Notwithstanding the contention, seriously offered in the literature, that "trees have interests," some viewpoints are very difficult to conceive of as interests, and thus difficult to represent in interest group negotiations where participants are described as stakeholders. Second, conceiving of participants in terms of their interests is most consistent with legal discourse, but nothing guarantees that the legal values of due process and natural justice will accompany the importation of legal discourse (stakeholders) into the regulatory arena.

Finally, conceiving of democracy as a bargaining process among interested parties, and of regulation as simply one venue where bargaining occurs, might satisfy some criteria for democracy, but it hardly exhausts the options. For many people, democracy is something other than (or more than) interest group negotiation. Democracy must incorporate widespread debate about issues of public concern. From this perspective, when regulation is viewed exclusively as interest group negotiation, and participation only in terms of stakeholders, democracy is seriously undermined.

Risk-benefit, Cost-benefit

All formal federal regulations are now subject to a regulatory impact assessment, but the introduction of new approaches to regulatory assessment extends beyond these formal requirements. Similar approaches — risk-benefit, cost-benefit and socio-economic impact assessment — are often used in setting informal rules, guidelines, policies and with respect to individual regulatory decisions. Sometimes these new approaches involve formal procedures — for example, hearings or requirements for extensive documentation. Other times, the new approaches to regulation are applied without a formal public process or legal requirements. In all cases, these new approaches have three elements in common.

First, implicit in risk-benefit assessment is a comparison: action is contrasted with the consequences of non-action (regulatory impact assessment); costs are weighed against benefits; potential results are weighed against the value of a proposed initiative (socio-economic or environmental impact assessment); health risks are compared to possible health benefits (risk-benefit). Note, however, that these comparisons are specific to the initiative being considered; they are not comparisons between different options for public policy. For example, public policies regarding health prevention, economic development or approaches to regulation are not considered, and for the most part, they are not intended to be considered in cost-benefit or similar methodologies. Second, all these comparative approaches assume that the relevant data can be quantified. For example, risk evaluation is premised on the quantification of risk estimates (e.g., a typical risk estimation is 10^{-6}). Quantifiable costs are even predicted for activities that have not yet commenced or of which there is no prior experience. Indicators —requirements for hospital beds or placements in alcohol treatment centres — are used to assess the social costs and benefits from economic development. Third, the new approaches are highly formulaic. They assume comparability among the various decisions faced by the regulator and are premised on the development of a uniform protocol to deal with different cases. Once the methodology has been developed, it is assumed that the task to be done is technical, routine, in nature.

To what extent can these new comparative approaches be combined with the democratic potential of regulation associated with co-management, direct democracy, due process, and delegated legislation? It is easily evident how different a risk-benefit or cost-benefit approach might be from the kind of policy debates occurring when regulators act as delegated legislators. Broad issues of public policy have little role to play in these comparative methodologies. Similarly, none of these comparative approaches can easily be linked to direct democracy. In each case, public contributions are intended to be limited in scope. More often it is intended that they be replaced by expert evaluations. Risk benefit is more easily linked to co-management inasmuch as regulators depend upon industry to generate both the proposals and the information required for regulatory assessment; but co-management in this case imposes significant burdens on industry (to generate the data), and it is consequently not always welcomed.

Less evident from this brief description, but easily documented through case studies, are the implications of these new approaches for the democratic potential of regulation arising from due process. The supposedly expert-based and formulaic orientation in cost-benefit or regulatory impact assessments often becomes highly adversarial in practice. Those whose viewpoints or interests are affected by the outcome lose little time before demanding participation and challenging the limitations of these new approaches and the formulas they use. Indeed, the methodologies of risk-benefit and other such methodologies have become as controversial as the regulatory decisions that result. It is easy for adversaries to draw upon disagreements among experts and to use these disagreements as a forum for conflicts about other than scientific or technical matters. In other words, the result of applying the new approaches — namely, cost-benefit, risk assessment, regulatory impact assessment and environmental assessment — is often that regulation embraces the worst attributes of adversarialism. Environmental assessments are good examples of "rampant proceduralism" on one hand, and of what happens when public debate is artificially constrained by the methodologies of regulation, on the other.

Regulatory Review

"Regulatory reviews" have become so commonplace in the last decade that some regulators feel that a line item should be added to their budget just to accommodate the recurrent demands. Most recently, some government departments have engaged in yet another regulatory review, designed to examine how their regulations affect competitiveness. In all these reviews, the basic premise is that regulation is inherently burdensome: there are too many regulations, too much record keeping and so on. These regulatory reviews are centred on "streamlining regulation," or more recently on achieving "smarter regulation," which is taken to mean achieving regulatory goals at lower cost to government as well as industry. The fact that regulation is often demanded by industry, and that it represents negotiation and compromise, is discounted. The detailed knowledge that regulators possess about the sector or issue they regulate is considered to have no intrinsic value. In other words, regulatory reviews are not associated with economic development strategies, even though is often now claimed in the literature that regulation can be used to promote competitiveness and economic development.

As they have developed in Canada, regulatory reviews are highly consultative. Indeed, in some departmental reviews, both the direction for and the methodology of these reviews is entirely based upon consultations with industry. Industry is expected to identify the burdens and problems of regulation. More consultation is both the objective of the review and the methodology for conducting it. On first impression, then, regulatory reviews are the exemplar of co-management. But because the purpose of regulatory review is to reduce regulation, "management" is an inappropriate term. Co-operation between the regulator and the regulated industry is directed to a single objective: achieving the least burdensome method of delivering the lowest level of regulation compatible with the legislative mandate of the regulator. Management of the relevant sector is not intended. Needless to say, regulatory reviews are seldom associated with due process or direct democracy. And given the basic premises upon which they operate, the reviews do not envision treating regulators as delegated legislators empowered to develop public policy in areas of their jurisdiction.

REGULATION TODAY: ITS POTENTIAL FOR DEMOCRACY

Assessing the democratic potential of regulation is a complicated task. Regulation is not democratic in the usual sense of the term. Yet, on occasion, regulation is highly democratic by almost any standard of judgement. This paper has explored a model for examining democracy in regulation, viewing regulation as a form of governance. It focused on four elements of governance in regulation — namely, co-management, direct democracy, due process and delegated legislation — to see both how they each support and potentially undermine the democratic potential in regulation. It suggested that the greatest potential for democracy might lie in the combination of all four elements of governance in regulation. Used in combination, each offers the possibility of off-setting some of the negative consequences of the others.

As is the case with all models, this argument is theoretical. Testing it in the practical context of regulation is a complicated task because regulatory regimes differ radically from one other. No analyst could hope to acquire adequate knowledge of the very many examples of regulation. The approach taken in this paper has been to focus on the keywords of the regulatory debate. Keywords were indicators of the general orientation of regulation, which is likely to be reflected in specific decisions and policies. This approach is necessarily only suggestive, but it can be related directly to case studies of regulation.

The keywords examined were "consultation," "stakeholders," "risk-benefit" and "regulatory reviews." The analysis of keywords suggests that the orientation of regulation to co-management has been strengthened in recent years, but the scope of co-management (i.e., the capacity to manage the sector and deal with its many problems) is now highly restricted. Although considerable emphasis was placed on due process provisions less than a decade ago (even in conjunction with proposals for deregulation and reform), the current practice of regulation generally de-emphasizes due process and legal norms. The exception is environmental regulation, which unfortunately has been subjected to adversarialism. Moreover, environmental regulation often deals with issues of broad public concern only when the legitimacy of the regulators is being challenged. In general, there is much evidence today that the policy-making functions of regulation — the capacity of regulators to function as delegated legislators — has also been curtailed. Furthermore those who wish to use regulation as a forum for debate of public issues are finding that it is necessary to conceive of themselves as stakeholders, or interested parties. Consequently, they are also finding the climate for public debate about regulatory issues quite chilling.

No one would dispute that there has been a sea change in regulation in the last decade. This paper has argued that the sea change also affects the democratic potential of regulation. Whatever potential exists for democracy in regulation as a form of governance, it has been curtailed by developments affecting the capacity of regulation to function as co-management, as a sphere of direct democracy, as an exemplar of the legal values of due process, and as a forum for debate about issues of public concern. Moreover, the balance among the various aspects of regulatory governance has changed so that, for example, co-management has been strengthened at the expense of due process and policy making. In other words, prospects for democracy in regulation are not currently very encouraging.

In retrospect, it should not have been surprising that a sea change in regulation generally also affects its democratic potential. If fault is to be found, it is that the connection between regulation and democracy was not explored adequately at the outset or during the recent period of regulatory reform. As a consequence, no one has paid much attention to the effect on democracy of regulatory reform programs. Putting democracy on the agenda in discussions about regulation is a necessary corrective. In all likelihood it will change the discussion about regulatory reform.

Regulatory reform and democracy in regulation are not antithetical. Needless to say, regulation need not be inefficient, a barrier to innovation, administratively hide-bound or rigid in order to be democratic. But unless attention is paid to the consequences of any reform proposals for democracy, the democratic potential of regulation is hardly likely to be strengthened. This paper will have served its purpose if it draws attention to the problem, and opens up the discussion.

1. See, for example, the Patent Medicines Prices Review Board or the various tribunals created in conjunction with copyright legislation.

2. R. Howse, Robert Pritchard and Michael Trebilcock, "Smaller or Smarter Government," *University of Toronto Law Journal,* Vol. 40, no. 3 (1990), pp. 498-541.

3. For an example of the types of concerns felt by legislators about regulation and the government's response to them, see Ministry of State (Privatization) and Minister Responsible for Regulatory Affairs, *Federal Regulatory Plan 1987* (Ottawa: Supply and Services, 1986).

4. For an assessment of the initial program for regulatory reform, see Robert O. Anderson, Margot Priest, W.T. Stanbury and Fred Thompson, *Government Regulation: Scope, Growth, Process* (Montreal: Institute for Research on Public Policy, 1980). Most of their recommendations have since been implemented.

5. For various descriptions of regulation and its multiple functions, see: Stephen Brooks and Andrew Stritch, *Business and Government in Canada* (Scarborough: Prentice Hall Canada Inc., 1991); John C. Strick, *The Economics of Government Regulation: Theory and Canadian Practice* (Toronto: Thompson Educational Publishing, 1990); William Coleman and Grace Skogstad (eds.), *Policy Communities and Public Policy in Canada: A Structural Approach* (Mississauga: Copp Clark Pitman, 1990); Harold Kaplan, *Policy and Rationality: The Regulation of Canadian Trucking* (Toronto: University of Toronto Press, 1989); Richard Schultz and Alan Alexandroff, *Economic Regulation and the Federal System* (Toronto: Royal Commission on the Economic Union and Development Prospects for Canada, 1985); and Canada, *Economic Instruments for Environmental Protection* (Ottawa: Supply and Services, 1992).

6. The exceptions are David J. Mullan, *Rule Making Hearings: A General Statute for Ontario* (Toronto: Ontario Commission on Freedom of Information and Individual Privacy, 1979) and Gregory Craven, *Public Policy Workshop on Consultation in Rule Making — Some Lessons from*

Australia (Toronto: University of Toronto Faculty of Law, 1990).

7. Michael J. Trebilcock, *The Choice of Governing Instrument* (Ottawa: Supply and Services, 1982).

8. For examples see Strick, *The Economics of Government Regulation*; Schultz and Alexandroff, *Economic Regulation.* For a different perspective, see Bruce Doern and Richard W. Phidd, *Canadian Public Policy: Ideas, Structure, Process,* 2nd ed. (Scarborough: Nelson Canada, 1992); Lloyd Brown-John, "Comprehensive Regulatory Consultation in Canada's Food Processing Industry," *Canadian Public Administration,* Vol. 28, no. 1 (Spring 1985), pp. 70-98.

9. For discussions of accountability in the context of Canadian regulation see: H. N. Janish, "Policy Making in Regulation: Towards a New Definition of the Status of Independent Regulatory Agencies in Canada," *Osgoode Hall Law Journal,* Vol. 17, no. 1 (1979), pp. 46-106; Kenneth Kernaghan, "Political Control of Administrative Action: Accountability or Window Dressing?" *Les Cahiers de Droit,* Vol. 17 (1976), pp. 927-34; Lucinda Vandervort, *Political Control of Independent Administrative Agencies: A Study Paper Prepared for the Law Reform Commission of Canada* (Ottawa: Law Reform Commission 1980); Economic Council of Canada, *Responsible Regulation: An Interim Report* (Ottawa: Economic Council of Canada, 1979).

10. See, for example: *Federal Regulatory Plan 1987*; Cassandra Blair, *Forging Links of Co-operation: The Task Force Approach to Consultation* (Montreal: Conference Board of Canada, 1984); James Gillies, *Facing Reality: Consultation, Consensus and Making Economic Policy for the Twenty-first Century* (Montreal: Institute for Research on Public Policy, 1986).

11. See, for example: Debora Mackenzie, "Europe Opens Environmental Data Up to Public Scrutiny", *New Scientist,* March 31, 1990, p. 24.

12. Michael, J. Trebilcock, "Regulation and the Consumer Interest: The Canadian Transport Commission's Costs Decision," *Canadian Business Law Journal,* Vol. 2 (1978), pp. 101-13; Michael J. Trebilcock, The Consumer Interest and Regulatory Reform," in Bruce J. Doern (ed.), *The Regulatory Process in Canada* (Toronto: Macmillan, 1978); David J. Mullan, "Natural Justice" and Bernard Coutois, "Intervenor Funding," in Neil R. Finkelstein and Bruce Macleod Rogers (eds.),

Recent Developments in Administrative Law (Toronto: Carswell, 1987).

13. John Mark Keyes, *Executive Legislation* (Toronto: Butterworths, 1992); Denys C. Holland, *Delegated Legislation in Canada* (Toronto: Carswell, 1989), especially chaps. 2-3; Cameron Hazelhurst and J. R. Nethercote (eds.), *Reforming Australian Government: The Coombs Report and Beyond* (Canberra: Australian National University Press, 1976); David J. Mullan, "The Impact of the Charter on Administrative Procedure: The Meaning of Fundamental Justice," in Ruth Kringle and Ross Nugent, *Public Interest v. Private Rights: Striking the Balance in Administrative Law, The 1990 Isaac Pitblado Lectures* (Winnipeg: Law Society of Manitoba, 1990).

14. Michael J. Trebilcock, "Winners and Losers in the Modern Regulatory System: Must the Consumer Always Lose?" *Osgoode Hall Law Journal,* Vol. 13, no. 3 (1975), pp. 619-47.

15. In Canada, the debate about regulatory capture has been taken up by Robert E. Babe, "Regulation of Private Television Broadcasting: A Critique of Means and Ends," *Canadian Public Administration,* Vol. 19, no. 1 (1976), pp. 552-86; C. Lloyd Brown-John, "Membership in Canadian Regulatory Agencies," *Canadian Public Administration,* Vol. 20, no. 3 (1977), pp. 513-33; and David A. Townsend, "An Examination of the Life Cycle/Capture Hypothesis and Its Potential Application to Canadian Independent Regulatory Agencies" (unpublished LLM thesis, Osgoode Hall Law School, 1982). There is some debate about whether "capture" is the appropriate term to describe what occurs in regulation. In this paper, it refers only the the exercise of undue or unchecked influence by industry on regulation.

16. An analysis of the contradictions in regulation can be found in Liora Salter, "Capture or Co-management: Democracy and Accountability in Regulatory Agencies," in Gregory Albo, David Langille and Leo Panitch (eds.), *A Different Kind of State? Popular Power and Democratic Administration* (Toronto: Oxford University Press, 1993); see also Andrew Roman, "Regulatory Law and Procedure," in Doern, *The Regulatory Process.*

17. See for example, Hudson N. Janisch, "Policy Making in Regulation," John Keyes, *Executive Legislation*; and Paul Verkuil, "The Purposes and Limits of Independent Agencies," *Duke Law Journal* (1988),

pp. 257-96. For a different approach to the same issue, see: H. W. Arthurs, "Regulation Making: The Creative Oportunities of the Inevitable," *Alberta Law Review,* Vol. 8 (1970), pp. 315-23.

18. For a comparison of different methods of regulation, see Liora Salter, "Methods of Regulation," study prepared for the Task Force on Broadcasting Policy (Ottawa: Supply and Services, 1986).

19. The author recently completed a study for Industry, Science and Technology Canada assessing regulatory reviews in five government departments.

20. Raymond Williams, *Keywords: A Vocabulary of Culture and Society* (London: Penguin, 1976).

21. Jacques Rousseau, "Regulatory Initiatives: The Legal Duty to Consult" (Ottawa: Library of Parliament, Law and Government Division, Research Branch, November 1, 1983).

22. Mullan, "Natural Justice," pp. 77-78.

23. Both Schultz and Alexandroff, *Economic Regulation,* and Brooks and Stritch, *Business and Government,* make a point of emphasizing the reciprocal relationships involved in regulation.

24. Susan G. Hadden, *A Citizen's Right to Know: Risk Communication and Public Policy* (Boulder: Westview Press, 1989). Hadden calls this situation "power sharing."

25. For a discussion of this, see Mullan, "Natural Justice."

26. Liora Salter, *Mandated Science* (Dordrecht/Boston: Kluwer Academic Press, 1988).

27. Robert Howse (ed.), *Topics in the Theory and Practice of Regulation,* Vol. 1. (Toronto: University of Toronto Faculty of Law, 1992-93); Kaplan, Policy and Rationality.

28. For a discussion of this, see Craven, *Public Policy.*

29. Canada, Parliament, Standing Joint Committee on Regulations and Other Statutory Instruments, Fourth Report, *Minutes of Proceedings and Evidence,* Issue no. 7, July 22, 1980, pp. 7-20.

30. R. MacDonald, "Judicial Review and Procedural Fairness in Administrative Law," *McGill Law Journal,* Vol. 25, no. 4 (1979), p. 523.

31. Rianne Mahon, "Canadian Public Policy: The Unequal Structure of Representation," in Leo Panitch (ed.), *The Canadian State,* 2nd ed.

(Toronto: University of Toronto Press, 1977).

32. Liora Salter, "Accountibility and Capture." See also Brooks and Stritch, *Business and Government,* who use a different term but make the same point.

33. For example, Gillies, *Facing Reality*; Blair, *Forging Links.*

34. Law Reform Commission of Canada, *Independent Administrative Agencies,* Report no. 26 (Ottawa: Supply and Services, 1985).

35. For a discussion of this, see Arthurs, "Regulation Making."

36. These limits are discussed, for example, in Robert L. Rabin, *Perspectives on the Administrative Process* (Boston and Toronto: Little Brown and Co., 1979).

S U S A N   D .   P H I L L I P S

W HOSE   D EMOCRATIC   P OTENTIAL ?

C OMMENTS   ON   L IORA   S ALTER ' S   P APER

There is no question that the relationship between governments and citizens is under pressure. The reforms related to enhancing democratic governance are as important to rethinking government as those aimed at improving efficiency and innovation. In fact, democratic reform under-pins the likelihood of the long-term success of attempts to reorganize and "reinvent" government because far-reaching change requires the acceptance of its principles and products by citizens. If the regime itself is not regarded as legitimate, responsive and accountable to citizens, it will be difficult to build support for structural, procedural or policy change.

The importance of Liora Salter's paper is that it analyzes both the democratic potential and limitations of regulation — an essential, but often overlooked aspect of governance. She makes the astute observation that, although regulation as a form of governance is not incompatible with democracy, recent changes in the regulatory process have strength-ened co-management (a reciprocal relationship among "stakeholders," usually industry and government, that places obligations on all parties to make compromises and to work together in a continuing relationship in order to "manage" the sector). This has come at the expense of due process and the capacity of regulators to function as delegated legislators.

Consequently, Salter argues, "prospects for democracy in regulation are not currently very encouraging."[1] There are several aspects of Salter's analysis that I would like to explore further. Specifically, attempts to enhance democratic governance must not only ask *how* citizens can (and do) participate in the process of governing, but *who* can (and does) participate? Does regulation have a differential effect on the opportunity of different types of stakeholders, citizens or groups of citizens to participate?

In contrast to many scholars of regulation who assert that the greatest limitation of the regulatory process is the likelihood of capture of the regulatory body or the overt co-optation of non-industry participants by the regulated industry or the process itself, I argue that a significant limitation on who participates and the extent to which they participate derives from the nature of knowledge demanded by the process. Regulation places a heavy emphasis on science, on making claims and counter-claims based on expert, defensible information; and thus, as Salter notes, it is often an adversarial process. Those ideas that cannot pass muster as scientific are merely consigned to the margins of public discussion. While they may be valued in other terms (as opinion, values or myth) they are not taken seriously as knowledge. As Salter indicates, this expertise bias is related to the heavy emphasis on risk-benefit analysis that focusses on specific regulations, rather than on more general policy options or alternative scenarios. In addition, should a group become involved in an ongoing process of co-management, it becomes extremely difficult to step outside the relationship to be a vocal critic without alienating the co-management partners. Thus, the opportunity to criticize becomes restricted the more deeply a group is involved in the regulatory process.

This process places tremendous pressure on interveners to act in a professional way. While technology — the availability of data banks and computer link-ups, for example — has given all groups greater access to information, the ability to produce expert information and act in institutional ways is more difficult for some types of groups than others. The groups that are most likely to be disadvantaged by the nature of this process are those representing social movements, such as women's, Aboriginal peoples, gay rights and disabled persons movements.[2] If playing the regulatory game in a particular way — being professional, legalistic and expert — is more likely to be successful, why would such groups not participate on these terms as they, too, like to win on public policy issues? Naturally, some simply may not have the financial resources, even if they act as coalitions, to be able to purchase expert information and testimony, hire lawyers or devote weeks of staff time to monitoring regulatory hearings. But, the answer is not one of resources alone. Rather, it rests on an understanding of how social movement politics differs from that of other interest groups.

In contrast to the way in which social movements often are portrayed by the political right, they are not narrowly focussed, self-interested "special interest groups." Rather, they are interested in the democratization of everyday life, including "private" institutions such as the family, workplace and church as well as the state. Both *representation* of interests and direct *participation* of individuals in social movements are important. There is real meaning for movement politics in the adage, "the personal is political and the political is personal." The concept of citizenship emphasized by these groups is one in which all citizens should have more or less equal opportunities to exercise the consumption of collective goods and services, and to enjoy the right to participate in the decision-making process that determines the allocation of the benefits (and costs) of public policies. This has resulted in a sense that people hold procedural rights — that consultation should not be presented merely as opportunities, offered or withdrawn at the discretion of government officials, but should be enjoyed as a quasi-right. Thus, for many such groups, being forced to act in a highly institutional, conventional way in which the most valued participants are the experts often involves important tradeoffs, sometimes forces significant organization transformations and, over the long term, risks undermining the very essence of their participatory, reflexive politics.

The difference between environmental and women's groups is instructive in this regard. Over the years, national environmental groups in Canada (as in the US) have become money-making machines. Large sums of money are necessary in order to buy the expertise to participate in Environmental Impact Assessment and other regulatory hearings. Thus, environmental groups devote a considerable time and energy to fundraising, and comparatively speaking, are quite good at it. But, this emphasis on expertise has had a price: membership and opportunities for participation by members in national environmental groups has severely atrophied, if they ever truly existed. In almost all cases, members are donors only, with little opportunity to participate in activities and policy making within environmental groups as organizations. In contrast, women's groups tend to place a heavy emphasis on membership participation probably at the cost of some measure of expertise and professionalism. In many cases, their fights are still highly political ones over values, not science, and over discourse, not specific regulations.

My thesis is that there exists a paradox in the current unfolding of enhanced democratic governance that, I argue, will disadvantage the representatives of social movements that do not become highly professionalized.[3] While there may be more opportunities for the representation of interests, such as regulatory hearings, royal commissions, legislative committees, "multi-stakeholder" consultations and ultimately "partnerships" or co-management arrangements, the *mode* or practice of representation is becoming increasingly constrained. The paradox is that while social movements (as important democratizing agents) gain greater access to policy making, there is greater pressure to behave in conventional, professional ways with an emphasis on representation over participation and with reduced tolerance for the expressive actions that are essential to their politics. Thus, as the tendency toward co-management grows in the regulatory process, social movements either undermine the very essence of their politics or they are excluded. Consequently, the new opportunities for participation may mean a more constricted range of players. And this ultimately works to the detriment of democracy.

MAKING REGULATION AND GOVERNANCE MORE DEMOCRATIC

While it would be improbable — and, indeed, counter-productive — to remove the emphasis on scientific information in regulation, the need to keep the process open to a wide range of players leads to two suggestions for supplementary measures.

First, we need to recognize that there is a problem in imposing democracy (which implies some measure of at least procedural equality) on an unequal society, because some people will count for more than others. Therefore, there is a strong case to be made for financial and other types of support for less advantaged groups so that they, too, can participate in policy formulation. This should take the form not only of intervener funding (which usually goes to already well established groups), but of ongoing organizational support for less advantaged groups. In Canada, we historically have offered such assistance under the guise of enhancing citizenship and have provided grants to a range of groups, including official language minority associations, women's groups, Aboriginal organizations, multicultural groups and disabled persons groups by the Secretary of State. We have also provided funding to other citizen groups through federal departments (and by other levels of government) and, on a more limited basis, have offered tax expenditures under the Income Tax Act to "charitable groups."[4]

However, in recent years, "special interest groups" — a term used inappropriately to include a wide range of social movements and citizen groups — have been targeted by the Conservative government as *the* problem of governing because they overload governments by placing too many, too varied and often irreconcilable demands on them. Federal budgets since 1990 have dramatically slashed funding to a wide range of citizen groups. While I am not suggesting that every group that asks government for money should receive it, I am arguing that by using groups as a scapegoat for the complexities of governing in the 1990s, we put ourselves in a contradictory position. Governments need an extensive array of interest groups to intervene at regulatory hearings and participate in consultations in order to produce policy that is regarded as legitimate and acceptable to citizens. Governments also need the expertise, in the form of both scientific and popular knowledge, resident in these groups. While we are asking groups to do more (to produce information, consult and provide community services), we are cutting off their resources and blaming them for many of the difficulties intrinsic to governing. My argument is that, rather than attacking social movements and citizen groups as part of the problem, we need to look at them as one potential solution in rethinking democratic government, and we need to find ways of encouraging their active participation in the regulatory process.

The second suggestion relates to the case which Salter makes that due process in regulation increasingly has come to be defined narrowly in legalistic and adversarial terms centred on a formal hearing process confined to stakeholders. The problem which emerges from this approach is that for many citizen groups without direct pecuniary interests in the issue, their stake may not be readily apparent to them because the issues have been defined by the other players and by the regulatory body in constricted, highly technical terms. While this may work to the advantage of the regulated industries because it contains the scope of potential conflict and range of players involved, it often precludes attaining a sense of how the regulatory issue at hand fits into the bigger picture of values and public policy. The absence of citizen groups at regulatory hearings, which may be mistaken for apathy, in reality may be a result of this narrowness of the definition of the issues.

The opportunities for participation by a wide array of groups could be extended if a pre-hearing communication and consultation process were instituted that would allow groups the chance to define their positions and set the regulatory question in the context of the broader set of related issues. For example, the Fair Tax Commission in Ontario spent considerable time in working groups and information sessions before going to public hearings. Without this consultation and learning phase, the hearing stage probably would be little more than gripe sessions about taxes without ever getting to consideration of different options and possibilities, or would involve a very restricted range of stakeholders with obvious and direct vested interests.

CONCLUSION

In conclusion, I offer an observation on factors that are likely to put new pressures on the democratization of regulation and a question on the democratic reform of governance in general. First, the observation. There are two emerging pressures that will affect regulation and its democratic potential that are not discussed in the paper by Salter. The notions of due process and fairness of representation are under pressure to address the issue of who participates. Increasingly, the social movements that I have been discussing hold a sense of procedural rights not only for participation by their own groups, but a responsibility to ensure that the diversity of society is represented. For example, the National Action Committee on the Status of Women (NAC) and several other groups withdrew their support for the federal Panel on Violence against Women not because they their own organizations were inadequately represented, but because they believed minority women in general were not well represented. This sense of quasi-rights to participate is not being exercised merely in the limited self-interest of individual organizations, but is being used by them as watchdogs over the process in general. The importance attached to the politics of inclusion and the sense of procedural rights exercised by social movements is likely to expand the concept of fairness and place an even greater onus on the state to ensure representation of a full spectrum of interests.

The second pressure stems from the international outlook and integration of many social movements. This has promoted the notion that there exists a global concept of citizenship which entails the protection of certain universal human, social, economic and environmental rights. This means that many groups expect governments to adhere to standards that are universal and international, rather than simply to those legislated by the nation-state. Therefore, many social movements are willing to call upon supranational institutions, other governments, foreign corporations or international conventions to get national governments to behave in particular ways. For example, Aboriginal peoples and the environmental movement have had some success in calling upon the United Nations, using the Law of the Sea Treaty or appealing to international summit conferences, to influence the Canadian and other governments to change their laws and policies which these movements argue are in violation of international laws, conventions and expectations. While governments still retain overwhelming control over the participatory aspect of regulation (and consultation in general) because they retain the power to determine who is a stakeholder and, thus, a legitimate player, the globalization of policy processes may pressure them to seek more extensive democratic reform.

Finally, my question. In some ways, democratic reform will be more difficult to achieve than those reforms related to improving productivity and innovation because inadequate attention is given to assessing success. How do we evaluate the success of democratic reform: by the numbers who participate; by who participated; by the product of the process, for example, whether compromise was reached; by acceptance by participants and non-participants that the process was a legitimate and fair one? Perhaps the first step on the road to enhancing the democratic potential of governance is to establish indicators that will tell us when we have arrived.

1.   Liora Salter, "Experiencing a Sea Change in the Democratic Potential
      of Regulation," this volume, p. 154.

2.   For an expansion of this line of argument see Susan D. Phillips, "New
      Social Movements and Routes to Representation: Science versus
      Politics," in Stephen Brooks and Alain-G. Gagnon (eds.), *Social
      Scientists, Policy Communities and the State* (New York: Praeger Press,
      1993).

3.   This analysis is drawn, in part, from Clause Offe, "The Separation of
      Form and Content in Liberal Democratic Politics," *Studies in Political
      Economy,* Spring 1980, pp. 5-16.

4.   For a discussion of funding of interest groups using tax expenditures
      see A. Paul Pross and Iain S. Stewart, "Lobbying the Voluntary Sector
      and the Public Purse," in Susan D. Phillips (ed.), *How Ottawa Spends
      1993-1994: A More Democratic Canada...?* (Ottawa: Carleton
      University Press, 1993), pp. 109-42.

SUMMARY OF DISCUSSION

One participant suggested that in both Liora Salter's presentation and Susan Phillips' commentary the use of the term "democracy" was contestable. Some groups representing different interests choose to claim rights (in the name of democracy) to consult but question their ability to be effective participants in (what they say is) a flawed process. How can groups that are active on an ongoing basis be compared with those that participate periodically? What are the limits and parameters by which we measure the legitimacy of participation? In effect, what does democracy mean and how do we evaluate the claims groups make?

Salter responded that contestability is the essence of democracy. From the perspective of regulators, the problem is to determine who precisely is the public to which they are to respond. Often, regulators do not know whom the groups represent, believing that simply to transport the debate carried on in Ottawa to outlying regions qualifies as consultation. Enhanced participation in regulation might create a debate that will inform policy makers and then legislators. It is essential for regulators to define what they want to achieve through regulation and then to set up the mechanism that will allow them to meet these goals.

On the question of democracy, Phillips responded that if groups do not participate in regulatory hearing processes, it is not because they are disinterested, but rather because they do not have the information to allow them to participate. Different groups have specific information and expertise that gives them a strong sense of ownership over an issue compared to political parties; therefore, these groups are important to the process. It is becoming increasingly important to ensure the legitimacy of the consultation process as more and more people are becoming sceptical of this same process. Perhaps a reexamination of the process might be one of the ways through which we can instill greater legitimacy into consultation.

A second participant noted that the roundtable began by examining what is wrong with the public sector; some participants implied the public sector would be fine were it not for the political process. The intervener suggested this is the wrong way to examine the situation: change can only occur through the political process. In fact, consultation and regulation are really the problems we are trying to correct. These are instances of government trying to micro-manage complex sectors, which is not ideal. The legitimacy of the political process is in effect a negative process, because we choose not to recognize the legitimacy of the political process at the outset. To call this whole process of consultation and regulation democratization is a tremendous compliment which will never be deserved.

Salter responded that in her estimation there is an integration between regulation and legislation. In regulation, the public and the political processes come together; there is a creative tension. She believes that there are possible ways of making regulation more democratic.

A third participant stressed that once regulation is in place we must make certain that it is effective. Now that we have a more open process of globalization, capital and money are essentially foot-loose and can escape regulation. Companies can threaten to move elsewhere to escape regulation. In order not to fall victim to these threats, we might need to make rules more flexible.

Salter responded that in the last ten years we have maintained that regulation is burdensome. However, we use regulation as a positive tool to help our firms compete. We have a mindset problem: we view regulation as being coercive instead of viewing it positively in the sense of being able to create a more potentially democratic process.

Phillips noted that we tend to think of globalization only in terms of economics; but it also has enormous political implications. First, globalization has led to more class division, individualism and a decline in the sense of political community. Second, there is more terrain for the internationalization of interests. In her view, governments are left with the responsibility of developing a sense of community.

REINVENTING LOCAL GOVERNMENT:

THE PROMISE AND THE PROBLEMS

D A V I D   S I E G E L

REINVENTING LOCAL GOVERNMENT:

THE PROMISE AND THE PROBLEMS

Canada has never experienced an "urban crisis," but this might be about to change. The lack of a crisis has had a significant impact on the development of the municipal system in Canada. Crises can pose major threats, but they can also bring forward opportunities for major changes.

The corruption in US cities at the turn of the century produced the council-manager form of government which has had a major impact on the way American cities have been governed. The racial unrest in American cities in the 1960s activated the "best and the brightest" practitioners and academics to devote themselves to searching for solutions to the "urban problem." The amount of attention focussed on cities created many changes in their operation.

In Canada, local governments have been victims of their success. With rare exceptions, municipalities have provided high levels of service at reasonable cost with very little fanfare. The lack of an urban crisis has meant that municipal government has been taken for granted. The only time people ever think about the water supply in their homes is when it is *not* there. The same can be said for most other municipal services. Municipalities have generally done such a good job of delivering services that people forget that they are there.

Without sounding too alarmist, a configuration of events is unfolding which might generate Canada's first urban crisis. As mentioned above, a crisis is also an opportunity. Local governments should be prepared to use the developing urban crisis to focus attention on the systemic problems that have always hindered local government administration.

This paper offers some suggestions for taking advantage of this developing crisis-cum-opportunity to improve the quality of urban governance. The first part of the paper discusses the *promise,* i.e., the contribution which local government could make to the process of rethinking government. The second part discusses the *problems* which local governments face in attempting to be flexible enough to be entrepreneurial and restructure themselves in the face of the impending crisis. The third section suggests a set of *prescriptions* to assist local governments to take advantage of the crisis, improving their governing mechanisms and management skills. The final section contains some *caveats* about getting so caught up in reinventing government that some of the important characteristics of the traditional role of government are forgotten. This last section is unabashedly old-fashioned in that it uses words like "public interest" and "clear lines of accountability" instead of "client-centred" and "entrepreneurial."

The general argument of the paper will be that much can and should be done to improve the operation of local government but that these improvements must be made without destroying such traditional concepts as accountability and concern for the public interest. This could well require limits on ideas like "entrepreneurship."

THE PROMISE

There is a strong feeling now that governments must change their method of operation. Traditionally, governments did two things: raised revenue and provided services. This meant that governments really had only two decisions facing them: to change revenue levels or change service levels. In the current climate of serious financial constraints this offered two possible directions: increase revenue or reduce services. Neither of these alternatives is really palatable to a citizenry which has come to expect much of government.

However, some people saw a different way out of this problem. If governments could be made to work smarter, then they could accomplish more with less revenue. This thinking has had at least two major manifestations. In the United States, David Osborne and Ted Gaebler wrote the book *Reinventing Government*[1] in which they urged public service managers to forget their bureaucratic ways and become more entrepreneurial. They suggested that governments should concentrate on *steering* the ship of state rather than *rowing*. Their analysis of the current malaise facing governments was that most government organizations had invested so many resources in rowing that they did not have enough left over to steer. Osborne and Gaebler's prescription was to encourage entrepreneurialism in government and to focus on the idea that government should be a catalyst and facilitator rather than a doer.[2] Government could accomplish more with fewer resources if it enabled and encouraged other organizations to act. Their plea for rethinking government was directed at all levels of governments, although most of the examples cited in their book come from local governments.

The second manifestation of a similar way of thinking arose at roughly the time in the United Kingdom. This applied most directly to local government and suggested that local governments should become "enabling authorities." Like the American approach, it focussed on encouraging local governments to work through other organizations and accomplish their goals by stimulating action on the part of others rather than engaging in direct provision of services.[3] The revised role of local government was to focus on articulating the overall needs of residents rather than responding to the desires of every interest group in providing a service.

Local government *could* provide a tremendous laboratory for testing ideas about innovation and entrepreneurship. In his book *Laboratories of Democracy*,[4] David Osborne focusses on several states in the US which have served as living laboratories conducting innovative experiments in public policy to guide other states. The significance of his title is that sub-national units in federations have a tremendous opportunity to innovate. They generally function on a much more manageable scale than the national government, which gives them more flexibility. If the innovations are successful, they can then be extended to other sub-national units. If the innovations are not successful, the problems generated are correctible without causing serious dislocations for the entire federation.

Local governments should also be able to function as laboratories to test innovations. In fact, local governments have been doing innovative things like contracting out and establishing partnerships without ever realizing that they were being innovative. The temerity of federal and provincial governments in describing these initiatives as innovative because *they* just discovered them recently speaks volumes about the neglect of local government in this country.

Local governments can be innovative because they are the smallest unit of government. This means that they can undertake pilot projects at fairly limited cost, and that the consequences of such a project going awry are fairly easily reversible. Local governments can also benefit from their simplified form of non-partisan government. Before new policies can rise to the surface in federal or provincial governments, they must run the gauntlet of partisan political and/or administrative bureaucratic processes guaranteed to grind out any little bit of innovation in an allegedly "new" policy. For example, faced with a crisis in medical care and a number of very innovative approaches to restructuring the system, it seems that the major issue in the next federal election will be whether we should return to the system of user charges of the pre-1980s era. This is not exactly leading edge thinking, but in large political campaigns in which so much is at stake, radical, leading edge thinking is dangerous. Local governments benefit from not having a coterie of officials whose job it is to prevent innovative ideas from arising.

The proximity of local governments to ordinary citizens also assists the innovation process. In federal or provincial governments, politicians tend to surround themselves with like-thinking advisers and so become isolated from ordinary citizens. In local governments, politicians facing pressing local issues will frequently find themselves across the table (literally) from people who are directly affected by the issues and whose thinking is radically different from their own. Innovation is more likely to emerge from this clash of diverse individuals than it is from the common melody sung by like-minded people.[5]

Anyone who has worked through some local issue with a citizens' group becomes aware very quickly that "ordinary people" know a tremendous amount about dealing with problems which affect their everyday lives. People who actually live with problems on a day-to-day basis can see creative solutions which elude sophisticated professional experts.

Local governments have also been forced to be innovative because of the revenue constraints they face. Local governments have control over only one major source of revenue — the property tax. And in most provinces, they must share this with school boards and other organizations. Because of the reliance on one, fairly inelastic source of revenue, local governments have been reluctant to increase their revenue rapidly. This means that local governments became innovative and entrepreneurial long before other governments. Local governments discovered cost recovery in areas such as arenas, electrical power, water and sewers long before senior governments began charging for public services.

The combination of these several factors provides local governments with the ability to be very innovative. However, this is not the norm for local governments in Canada. Osborne and Gaebler's book, *Reinventing Government*, contains many examples of innovative and entrepreneurial local government activity in the US. A similar book in Canada would be much shorter.

The main source of identifying innovative programs in Canada has been the Institute of Public Administration of Canada's annual Awards for Innovative Management.[6] Local governments have been prominent in winning these awards in spite of the fact that they have been significantly under-represented in total entrants.[7] This indicates that local governments *can be innovative when they want to be,* but they have tended not be as innovative as senior levels of governments.

THE PROBLEMS

There are a number of reasons why local governments have not delivered nearly as much as they could have in terms of innovation. The impediments to reinventing government at the local level will be examined under three headings — structures of governance, collective action, and management. However, the first item on the agenda is a discussion of the impending crisis in local government, which will likely bring these three problems to the forefront.

As discussed earlier, there has always been a perception that local government has functioned well in this country. It has always been able to stay close to the people and provide services at the desired level. The current crisis is developing because citizens' expectations of local governments are increasing at the same time that the resources available to local governments are decreasing. The financial side of the problem facing local government has several elements. The limited ability of most local governments to raise their own funds makes them vulnerable to decisions made by other governments.

The federal government's decision to reduce its program expenditures has had a significant impact on local governments. The federal decision to reduce transfer payments to the provinces has caused provinces to pass those cuts along to local governments. Local governments are at the bottom of the ladder; they must simply absorb the cuts or increase taxes. Most local governments have done some of both, incurring a certain cost in terms of citizen dissatisfaction.

Provincial governments have also approached their financial problems by downloading certain responsibilities to local governments. In Ontario, the provincial government is planning to download responsibility for the entire property assessment function and for some roads.

Reductions in some federal and provincial programs have literally moved needy citizens from queues at federal and provincial offices to queues at city halls. Tougher federal unemployment insurance regulations have simply increased municipal social assistance rolls.

The second prong of the developing crisis in local government stems from changes in citizen expectations and in the nature of citizen involvement in the governing process. Increased levels and sophistication of citizen participation have considerably complicated the governing process. The raucous and unsophisticated citizen participation of the 1960s was fairly easily turned aside. The more sophisticated, middle-class citizen participation of the 1990s, frequently based on recently established legislative entitlements, is more complicated to handle.

Good citizen participation should improve both the decision-making process and the quality of decisions made, but it will also lengthen and complicate the decision-making process. Not only have traditional geographically based residents group become more vocal, but a number of new kinds of groups organized on the basis of ethnic origin, religion, gender, sexual orientation, and so forth are now becoming increasingly more well-organized and vocal. These groups clearly have a right to have their interests considered, but the increasing number of such groups lengthens and complicates the decision-making process.[8]

In some cases, groups use a municipal forum to present their views because it is close at hand and easy to manipulate, even though the issue at hand is not a municipal concern. Controversies over whether the Macedonian flag can be flown in the civic square or a beauty contest can be held on city property deal with issues which transcend local government, but dealing with these issues takes a great deal of energy, and deflects time and attention from real local government concerns.

In sum, the impending urban crisis is being caused by multi-faceted contradictory pressures. On the one hand, citizen pressures are encouraging local governments to do more at the same time that those pressures are slowing down the decision-making process. On the other hand, financial restraints are preventing local governments from responding to these pressures. If these pressures were straining against a municipal system which was in excellent condition, the system could probably stand the pressure. However, this pressure is being applied to a municipal system which has been functioning fairly well, but which has some weaknesses which the impending crisis will likely intensify.

Structures of Governance

Most provinces have too many, too small local governments. While small is beneficial in some ways for encouraging innovation, excessively small size causes several problems. Many local governments encompass such a small area and are so hemmed in by other governments that their scope for action is very limited. Both economic development and land use planning are highly problematic for small communities on the fringe of major urban areas.

The fiscal base of these small governments is also problematic. Their weak financial position makes it impossible for them to accumulate adequate resources to have enough slack in the system to experiment. Innovative activity always carries a certain risk. With absolutely no slack, these governments are unwilling to take even the slightest risk.[9]

The size problem has been addressed by some provinces by creating two-tier governments which group these smaller units of local government under a larger regional or metropolitan government. These have had mixed success. The larger governments are able to capture economies of scale and engage in more comprehensive land-use planning. They have also added a layer of government (with some attendant cost) and made the local government system more complicated for citizens to understand.

However, the major structural impediment to innovation by municipalities is the current form of provincial control of their activities. Provincial control of municipal government is a constitutional fact and it has a number of highly beneficial consequences. The problem is not the *fact* of provincial control; the problem is the *detailed method of control* employed by most provinces. Municipal governments can only engage in those activities which have been delegated to them by the provinces. In accomplishing this delegation, provinces can proceed along two paths. They could provide a general grant of power to deliver certain services within fairly broad perimeters to ensure that municipal actions do not subvert provincial policies. This is roughly the manner in which powers are divided between federal and provincial governments. Or, they could exercise detailed control over the process of most municipal activities. Too many provinces have opted for the latter alternative.

The detailed control has stifled the initiative of local governments. Not only does this totally preclude many actions, but it also creates a climate of caution and inertia. When a new idea is proposed, the first comment is not likely to be "Will it improve our organization?" or "Will it allow us to serve our residents better?" The more usual comment is "Check with the solicitor to see if we are allowed to do this," or "How will the province react if we do this?" The reason for this provincial predilection for detailed control can be found in the organization of provincial governments. Graham Allison has reminded us that governments are not monolithic entities.[10] Instead, they are made up of a loose collection of operating departments, each with its own set of goals and priorities.

Thus, provincial governments are composed of departments of municipal affairs which are concerned about the municipal system of government as a whole, and a number of other departments which view municipal governments as simply decentralized service delivery agencies only slightly different from their own regional and district offices.[11] This affects municipalities because the loose coalition of departments referred to as the "provincial government" can send highly conflicting signals to local governments.

The provincial departments which view local governments as service delivery agencies deal with local governments by continually narrowing their scope for independent action. They use such mechanisms as directives, provincial standards, and conditional grants to limit the initiative of local authorities. This is not done out of malevolence. It is done because the provincial ministries are charged with delivering a service (not maintaining a system of local government) and the best way to ensure that the service is delivered in the appropriate manner is by exercising detailed control over the service delivery organization.

Traditionally, departments of municipal affairs have carried less influence in the overall provincial government structure than other departments with larger programs and considerably more money to spend. This means that the only provincial department which is oriented to the municipal system of government as a whole takes a back seat to the departments which view municipal governments as decentralized provincial service delivery agencies.

When one views provincial governments as a collection of interests, it should not be surprising that local governments feel that they are receiving conflicting signals from provincial government departments. The more local governments become confused about the provincial government's overall direction, the more they become uncomfortable acting on their own.

This method of provincial organization is then mirrored at the local level. Given the relatively small size of most local governments, it would seem likely that they could be managed in a much more unified, corporate way than the larger provincial governments. This style of management would promote innovation because it would encourage managers to work together across departmental and professional boundaries to deal directly with the needs of clients.

In fact, it is very difficult for a council or a mayor or a chief administrative officer to take control and manage a municipal government on a corporate basis because most department heads have their own sources of funds through conditional grants and their own source of power through provincial directives, limiting the scope of municipal decision making in the provision of some services.[12] It is not unusual for a municipal council wanting to re-order its priorities to be told that it cannot eliminate a particular program because it is mandatory or that it cannot revise certain operating procedures because there are provincial standards. Local governments could be used as a mechanism to coordinate the delivery of provincial services at the local level,[13] but the nature of the provincial delegation of power prevents local governments from doing this.

These structural problems make it very difficult for municipalities to innovate in any meaningful way. First, they cannot venture into new areas without provincial approval. Provincial delegations of responsibility prescribed in very detailed ways are obviously more restrictive than general mandates to act in certain areas. Second, even if municipalities wanted to undertake innovative activities, they might not be able to find enough untied funding to allow then to shift their priorities.

Collective Action

The above discussion should not be taken to suggest that municipalities are totally without any influence on their environment. Municipalities have both national and provincial associations to represent their interests. In some provinces, there are a fairly large number of associations. The two major types of associations are the "political" associations (i.e., associations of municipal politicians) and administrators' associations. In some provinces, each of these major divisions is further divided. Some political associations group municipalities of like size or location, while the administrators' associations are frequently divided by professional specialty. It seems clear that municipalities have the capacity to look after their own interests, but how well does the system actually work?

It is quite normal for an association or interest group in any field to have a certain amount of difficulty satisfying all the needs of a diverse clientele. This problem is especially serious for municipal associations.

First, the membership is very diverse, usually ranging from the largest metropolitan areas in the province with strong manufacturing and commercial interests to the smallest residential hamlets in isolated rural areas of the province. These different entities have very different perspectives on almost every issue, making it very difficult for an association to speak with a united voice. The second problem is that, in spite of protestations to the contrary, these members are usually involved in zero-sum games. Functions conferred on counties or regions are not available to lower-tier municipalities; funds provided to urban areas are not available to rural areas. Association officials trying to negotiate agreements which are fair to all members experience a great deal of difficulty. This problem is exacerbated by the fact that some members can represent their own interests at least as well as the association can speak for them. This is the case for the largest cities in the province and for a few other cities with strong MLAs or other unique strengths.

Finally, there are times when these associations disagree with one another, further weakening the ability of municipalities to represent their own interests. For example, the Ontario government and the Association of Municipalities of Ontario began negotiations to "disentangle" or simplify a very complicated system of conditional and unconditional grants.[14] The Ontario Good Roads Association became concerned that this could result in the elimination of conditional grants for roads.[15] The resulting fight culminated in a nasty and public argument about who *really* represents municipalities.[16]

This kind of division makes it very difficult for municipalities to represent their own interests. Some municipal representatives allege that provincial governments use this division to impose their will on municipalities. However, local governments are frequently their own worst enemy. Their inability to agree on a preferred course of action forces the province to make its own decisions, which might be unsatisfactory to all the actors.

This analysis is not meant as a criticism of the associations. The problems are not the result of the intransigence of particular individuals; they reflect some very serious structural differences between the interests of different types of municipalities and interests within municipalities. It is difficult to think of another type of interest group with such a diverse clientele. These divisions weaken the ability of municipal governments to make their collective case with the provincial government and the same divisions also make it difficult for municipalities to cooperate with one another.

Management

The quality of municipal management in Canada is very high. This is surprising, given the almost complete lack of a systematic career development program for senior municipal managers and especially chief administrative officers.[17]

In the US, the widespread adoption of the council-manager style of government had a profound effect on municipal management and on the development of municipal managers. City management does not possess all the characteristics of a classical profession, but it has many of the trappings.[18] A student can study city management in a university program, such as the famous one at the University of Kansas, and come out equipped to be a generalist municipal manager[19]. Her or his first position is likely to be as an assistant in a city manager's office. From there the progression is on to being an assistant city manager, then a city (or town) manager in a smaller municipality, and up the ladder by moving to larger cities over time.[20] In this system, there is a full career path for someone trained as a generalist manager right from entry level to retirement. This also means that someone moving into a position as a city manager has had quite a bit of experience as a generalist manager before acceding to the top spot.

By contrast, the typical chief administrative officer (CAO)[21] in a Canadian local government has worked her[22] or his way up through the ranks of a major department, usually, public works or treasury.[23] He or she will seldom have had experience outside that "home" department. Managers moving from this specialized background into the position of chief administrative officer experience some initial difficulties in two dimensions.[24]

First, there is the problem of spanning many functions, most of which the new manager will have only a rather limited knowledge. Even when the manager does her or his best to be sensitive to the concerns of all these functions, there is almost always a lingering doubt that a "public works man" (for example) can deal even-handedly with all services.

Most organizations are conscious of the need to ensure that aspiring general managers have a good knowledge of all facets of the organization's activities. Therefore, it is usually considered an integral part of a manager's development to move through positions in all the major departments. The impermeable walls erected around municipal departments by professional groups generally limit this kind of movement in municipal administration. In the municipal world, career progression is usually seen as a straight line movement up the supervisory and managerial ladder supervising larger numbers of employees at each step. Movement to another department, particularly a staff function, would be regarded as an unfortunate digression rather than a learning experience.

The second difficulty facing CAOs is the need to learn very quickly the political aspects of dealing with a council. Department heads have some contact with council, but these are usually much simpler and more uni-dimensional than the relationship between council and the CAO. Again, other organizations have ways of preparing aspiring senior managers for these positions. Federal and provincial governments have central agencies such as the cabinet office or budget office through which managers pass to broaden their experience and to sensitize them to dealing with their political masters.

Few cities have analogous organizations which would provide that breadth of experience. Some CAOs have their own staff, but these tend to be fairly junior positions. In many cases, these positions are considered temporary, orientation kinds of positions, useful until the incumbent finds a "real job" in a department. Middle and senior level employees are seldom rotated through these positions as a part of their career development.

What all this adds up to is that Canadian cities have no systematic way to train and development generalist managers. The first experience that most municipal managers will have as a generalist manager is when he or she is appointed CAO. It is a bit like learning to swim by being thrown into the deep end. It is difficult to polish your stroke when you are expending all your energy figuring out how to survive.

The newly-appointed CAO must quickly learn how to "manage up" as well as "manage down."[25] "Managing down" refers to the traditional role of a senior manager in managing those beneath her or him in the hierarchy. Senior managers are usually fairly well equipped to handle this, although a frequent criticism of professional training is that it does not usually include training in how to be a manager.

"Managing up" involves managing the relationship between the manager and council. This is considerably more difficult than "managing down." First, it is not the neat hierarchical relationship that is involved in "managing down." Both the council and the CAO have certain legitimate bases of power, and they must learn to respect one another's turf. Second, councils seldom send clear and unequivocal signals to managers. Local government managers must become proficient at surmising what council really wants based on these very unclear signals.

But the greatest problem is that very little in a manager's background prepares her or him for "managing up." Managers spend their entire careers progressively moving up the ladder and gaining experience at "managing down." Then when they arrive at the top of the ladder, they must suddenly take on the new role of "managing up" for which they have no previous experience.

Most Canadian cities are very well-managed. Traffic flows well; buildings and parks are well-maintained; social programs are delivered reasonably well, given expenditure constraints. What is generally lacking, compared to the cities discussed in Osborne and Gaebler's *Reinventing Government,* is an innovative component to the manager's approach. Most senior managers arrive at their positions with a great deal of experience in making the existing services run well, i.e., "managing down." However, the fact that they have very limited experience in "managing up" means that they have to struggle with this a bit more than their American counterparts who have a different professional background.

Therefore, Canadian municipal managers are less comfortable at innovating than their American counterparts for two reasons. First, their specialist, professional background means that they are more likely to see municipal services as falling into water-tight compartments. They are unable to make the connections across services required for innovation. Second, lack of previous experience at "managing up" before assuming a senior position means that their first task in office is struggling with learning that role rather than innovating. Newly-appointed managers usually have a "honeymoon" period with council, i.e., a time at the beginning of their term when they have a great deal of support from council to make changes. A manager without previous experience "managing down" can use most of the honeymoon learning this skill.

George Vance undertook an extensive analysis of the managerial style of CAOs in Ontario municipalities. His work indicated that these managers were most oriented toward and most comfortable with "managing down." They put considerably less emphasis on "managing up."[26] The obvious prescription here, which will be developed at greater length in the next section, is that we need to hire and develop a new kind of manager.

PRESCRIPTIONS

Reinventing government requires a qualitatively different kind of local government than we have had in Canada. It requires moving toward what in Britain has been described as the "enabling authority," i.e., moving from "being a direct provider of services to stimulating, facilitating, enabling and monitoring."[27] This new type of authority will not focus narrowly on providing a limited number of mandated services, but will instead be concerned about the overall welfare of its residents. Thus, its role will involve interacting with a number of different organizations to ensure that a variety of services are provided rather than directly providing a more limited range of services. Some have compared this style to the French *communes,* which have very little power vested in them, but whose mayor is expected to persuade other governmental and non-governmental organizations to provide services to residents of the *commune*.[28]

There are already examples of this kind of enabling authority in Canada, but they are relatively limited. Quebec's new regional economic development strategy suggests that government should become the "partner state" rather than the "provider state."[29] Specifically, the government of Quebec is establishing a number of "regional councils" which will have small budgets, but whose major role will be to:

- ensure concerted action among players;
- advise the government;
- identify regional priorities and means of development;
- reach specific agreements with government departments and agencies to carry out actions provided for in the master agreement;
- ensure coordination and follow-through of development actions and programs in their area;
- manage, along with the Minister responsible for Regional Affairs, a regional development fund provided by the government to each region.[30]

Virtually all of these activities involve enabling, encouraging, and working through other organizations; the only mention of actually spending money was in the last item. This arrangement is likely a portent for all governments.

Structures of Governance

Provincial governments need to have a serious look at the structure of local government, but before that they should have a look at their own organizational structures. Part of the difficulty facing municipal governments is that the agency which speaks for them in the provincial government, municipal affairs, is usually a fairly weak department. This is because these departments tend to be small in terms of both human resources and budget, and limited in the scope of their operations. This, in turn, usually means that their minister is of relatively junior rank.

These weaknesses make it very difficult for municipal affairs, which is the only provincial department concerned with the municipal system as a whole, to deal on even terms with the large number of departments that see municipalities as service delivery agencies. It is premature to judge what might eventually come out of the disentanglement exercise in Ontario, but the indications are that the Ministry of municipal affairs is having a great deal of difficulty convincing such strong operating ministries as Transportation to give up their conditional grants. If provincial governments are really concerned about the governance of their municipalities, then they must find ways of increasing the status of departments of municipal affairs. This could come about through the appointment of higher profile ministers or the forced movement of conditional grants from other ministries to municipal affairs. At one time, Ontario moved the municipal affairs function into a large department called Treasury, Economics and Intergovernmental Affairs. At that time, municipal affairs officials felt that they has some additional status conferred by their combination with the very important treasury function. Some change in the structure of municipal affairs departments could improve their ability to represent municipalities at the provincial level.

The suggestion that provincial governments need to have a serious look at the structure of their local governments might sound surprising since some provinces seem to be constantly reviewing their local government structures. However, most of these reviews involve tinkering at the margins. They are usually driven by minor problems in the *status quo.* Thus, most time is spent on such issues as municipal boundaries, election dates, and number of councillors.

Provincial governments rarely ask themselves: "How can our local governments become more mission-oriented and value-driven?" And even when they pretend to ask those questions, the answers usually involve incremental rather than basic changes. Like most other organizations, provincial departments of municipal affairs are so busy dealing with pressing, day-to-day issues that they have difficulty standing back and reviewing the basic underpinnings of the system.

The first structural fix would be to look at the number and size of local governments. It is axiomatic among political scientists that small units of local government further local democracy. This has a great deal to recommend it in terms of citizen involvement. However, local democracy is not well served if governmental units are so small that they do not have the capacity to deliver the services desired by citizens. The key question is participation in the government of what? A parish council is impeccably democratic but may be incapable of doing anything of any importance. Some sort of balance has to be struck between functional capacity and the requirements of democracy.[31]

The second structural element that provincial governments should re-consider is their method of control of municipal activity. They must do this with the recognition that *provincial control of some aspects of municipal activity is absolutely essential.* For example, provincial control over the financial integrity of municipalities assists all municipalities by instilling greater confidence in municipal debt which results in lower interest rates. However, provincial governments should rethink the *manner* in which they have exercised their control. First, they should exercise restraint in moving too quickly in always correcting every alleged problem. The current feeling seems to be that if anything goes awry in any one municipality, then a regulation needs to be brought in covering every municipality. Provincial governments have been too much inclined to react to every presumed wrong identified by a citizens' group. They have been too little inclined to allow local governments reasonable amounts of autonomy to innovate and make their own decisions. It is quite normal in a democracy that some groups will be aggrieved about the actions of the majority; that does not always mean that some corrective action needs to be taken.

Second, the method of interaction between the provincial and local governments should move away from detailed controls to the provision of more general mandates or what is called in Europe "general competence."[32] Instead of detailed controls, provinces should specify the nature of provincial concern in a particular area and allow municipalities to do whatever they want within those boundaries.

A recent Ontario Royal commission on planning has recommended that provincial controls over municipal planning operate on the basis that the province defines its interest in advance in a particular geographic area and local governments are then free to make any planning decisions they want within those perimeters.[33] This would replace the existing system in which local governments propose planning measures and *then* discover that there is a provincial interest involved or they discover that the provincial government wants to protect the municipality from making what the province perceives as a mistake, even if there is no provincial interest at stake. Under the proposed system, local governments would be free to be as innovative as they want (including making their own mistakes) within those boundaries. This would encourage the idea that local governments have the expertise and maturity to make their own decisions and allow them to be innovative, while at the same time protecting legitimate matters of provincial concern.

In *Reinventing Government,* Osborne and Gaebler argue that governments are so busy rowing that they cannot steer. There is an exact analogy here with the workings of the planning system in Ontario. There is now approximately a one-year backlog of appeals of municipal planning decisions pending before the Ontario Municipal Board. Many of these are minor matters in which it is difficult to determine what the provincial interest is. If the above recommended changes are accepted, the province could withdraw from many of these minor matters and focus its full attention on the limited number of areas which are of provincial concern.

Provincial governments should exercise control over municipalities by defining clearly those areas which are of provincial concern and extending to municipalities an opportunity to make their own decisions as long as they do not conflict with those concerns. Some of the items which fall within the category of legitimate provincial interest are:

- general integrity of the municipal system, e.g., conduct of elections, conflict of interest;
- financial integrity of the municipal system, e.g., control over debt issuance; and
- preservation of lands and works of general provincial interest, e.g., historic areas, unique natural areas, agricultural lands.

In moving from detailed to more general controls, Canadian provinces might benefit from a review of the free local government experiment begun in Sweden in 1984, but now being implemented in other Scandinavian countries.[34] This allows individual municipalities to apply to be exempt from existing control legislation so that they can experiment with innovative ways of delivering services. They must present an overall plan of action which is approved by the national ministry. This could be viewed as a form of IMAA (Increased Ministerial Authority and Accountability) for local governments.[35]

Collective Action

The problem of improving collective action is much more difficult. As mentioned earlier, this is not a problem of the attitudes of a few individuals; the problem stems from the innate difficulty of balancing the interests of a large number of municipalities with very different needs and resources. Some provinces have one municipal association with a high level of intra-associational tension stemming from the conflict among different kinds of municipalities. Other provinces have several associations with less intra-association tension, but a high level of inter-association tension. It is unclear whether one arrangement is superior to the other.

However, it is clear that it is in the long-term interest of all munici-palities to have a strong municipal association with the power to deal strongly with the province. This will never develop as long as some municipalities prefer to do an "end-run" around the association to deal directly with the province. Municipalities should understand that it is in their long-term interest to restrain their tendency to break ranks over every short-term battle. This will strengthen the municipal association. Provincial governments should also exercise restraint in agreeing to deal with individual municipalities. Municipal associations will be strength-ened if ministers make the point that they deal with the association, not individual municipalities.

Management

Managing an innovative, enabling authority will be more complicat-ed than managing the traditional local government. Managers must con-tinue to be able to "manage up" and "manage down," although the latter role will be different with a reduced complement of more professional managers. However, the major change is that managers of the enabling authority must learn to "manage out," i.e., accomplish objectives by working through all sorts of outside agencies. This approach to govern-ing will need a very different style of manager from that of the tradition-al type of manager who has worked in Canadian local governments. In Vance's study of managerial approaches, he found that most CAOs sel-dom looked outward, and that when they did it was usually to provincial departments and other governments, and rarely to non-governmental organizations.[36]

Municipalities should be more conscious of the need to develop three types of managers — specialists, generalists, and enablers. This does not literally mean that there must be three different types of managers. Some managers will possess two or three traits, although they will be exceptions.

First, there will always be the need for specialist managers who are very knowledgeable about specific services. Discussions of the enabling authority usually focus on enabling and encouraging and only mention monitoring service delivery in passing if at all. In fact, the monitoring function will become very important. Local governments must be assured that the outside organizations with whom they are dealing are competent and are providing the service appropriately. Consumer satisfaction can be relied on for some feedback, but this can never replace monitoring by a competent professional. When the city of Phoenix decided to contract out its garbage collection, it also made the decision that it would always retain a limited garbage collection service internally. This meant that the city would never be totally dependent on outside organizations and that it would maintain some benchmark by which to compare the outside organizations.[37] Local governments moving toward the enabling mode should not forget this lesson. If local governments become *purely* enablers, they will lose their detailed expertise to monitor what others are doing. Therefore, there will always be a need for specialist managers, although there will probably not be a need for as many of them are there are today.

Second, local governments need to be conscious of the need to develop generalist managers, i.e., people qualified to be chief administrative officers. While there are now good generalist managers in the local government system, there is little evidence that this has come about through a conscious plan. Local governments need to do a number of things to encourage the systematic development of generalist managers. Some of these can be done internally. Managers should be encouraged to move laterally between departments at various stages in their careers so that when they become senior managers they have experience in a number of functional areas. This will require battering down some very tough professional barriers. It will likely not happen without a fight, but senior managers should be aware that it needs to be done.

Chief administrative officers should develop new organizational structures which provide staff members with a broader range of experiences *at all stages of their careers.* This could include developing a capacity to do policy analysis within the CAO's office. This would provide both a counterweight to analysis being done within departments and an avenue for managers to develop generalist expertise.

Finally, educational institutions and staff associations need to work together to provide developing generalist managers with the appropriate academic background. Most staff associations are organized along professional lines so that they provide educational programs which further the specialist aspects of a manager's career. There are now a few organizations, such as the Maritime Municipal Training and Development Board and the Ontario Municipal Management Institute, which will assist managers in developing a career path which could lead to being a generalist manager. These organizations need to be accorded greater recognition and there need to more of these types of organizations devoted to the training and development of generalist managers.

Educational institutions also need to do more than they have been doing. There are currently a very limited number of academic programs that provide academic programs directed at generalist municipal managers. These are usually geared to the mid-career manager. The only Canadian equivalent to the US programs which train generalist managers is the new MA in Public Administration program at the University of Western Ontario. This program provides a generalist education to both mid-career public servants and younger students. This is a promising initiative, but it is so new that it is impossible to assess whether local governments will actually be interested in hiring people who do not fit neatly into the traditional functional specialties. Even for mid-career people there are few generalist managerial positions below the CAO level.

Academics have been slow to develop these programs because there is a presumption that local governments will only employ entry-level people who have what is usually described as a "day-one skill," e.g., accounting, engineering, planning. If local governments are interested in hiring entry-level generalist managers, then more programs could be developed to cater to their needs. Alternatively, more should be done for mid-career managers to assist them in the tough move from being a functional specialist to being a generalist manager.

SOME CAVEATS

Osborne and Gaebler's book, *Reinventing Government,* has been an overwhelming success. It was a breath of fresh air which arrived at just the right time. Government employees had been aware for some time that their organizations were not working as well as they should and Osborne and Gaebler provided them with some illustrations of what other people have done to transform their organizations. However, there are some caveats that need to be considered before fully embracing the innovative, entrepreneurial view of government.

Clients, Entrepreneurs and the Public Interest. The literature on reinventing government and government as an enabling institution has grown rapidly and with good reason. Too often the stereotype of government employees who do not have time to serve the public because they are too busy filling out forms for no reason is very apt. This has caused many government employees to become time-servers rather than taking an interest in the quality of service delivered. There are many cases where it is clear that government organizations have served their employees better than they have served their clients.

However, a focus on promoting the innovative, entrepreneurial view of government should not overlook the fact that the role of government is to serve the broad public interest. This new style of government could develop into a government composed of a number of entrepreneurial institutions each doing its utmost to satisfy its clientele without regard to other interests. The danger in this kind of government is that it will be responsive to the best organized and most vocal interests at the expense of others. Gerry Stoker calls this the dual welfare system in which

> those who can afford it or who have the necessary skills acquire good-quality services in the private sector or in the market place of the public sector. Those without the necessary funds or skills are forced to rely on a basic no-frills state system.[38]

Caveats must also be registered about "entrepreneurship." If it means tossing out some of the silly, over-weaning central controls that governments have developed over the years and becoming more mission-oriented, then it is obviously a step forward. However, entrepreneurship has also been used as an excuse to develop private fiefdoms presided over by benevolent (or sometimes, not so benevolent) entrepreneurs. Looking at the role of a particular "bureaucratic entrepreneur" from two perspectives can be most enlightening.

Eugene Lewis has discussed in detail the lives of three "public entrepreneurs," one of whom was J. Edgar Hoover.[39] Hoover was plucked out of the Department of Justice as a young man to establish the Federal Bureau of Investigation because he was the only honest person who could be found. He built an honest and efficient police force which was the envy of many other jurisdictions. However, over time his entrepreneurship led him to see the FBI in a proprietary way and he used it as his private fiefdom, arbitrarily deciding to investigate non-criminals whom he disliked and ignoring apparent criminals for reasons which are still unclear.[40] Thus, "his" organization responded to his personal desires and not the rule of law or the broader public interest.

It is true that this is an extreme case because it involves a police force and because, well, J. Edgar Hoover was J. Edgar Hoover, enough said. However, while this case is extreme, it is not totally atypical. Students of local government will be familiar with the positive and negative aspects of the career of another of Lewis' entrepreneurs — Robert Moses.[41] And almost everyone who has studied government is aware of a case where an entrepreneur was able to overstep the bounds of accountability because of her or his entrepreneurial skills.

This is not an argument against some of the more positive aspects of entrepreneurship discussed earlier. However, it is a reminder that the greatest difficulty is not simply establishing a climate for entrepreneurship, but tempering that entrepreneurship with a respect for proper accountability and concern for the public interest.

Losing the Capacity to Control. The new perspective on reinventing government talks about the enabling authority or about more emphasis on steering than rowing. Clearly, governments could accomplish more with less if they focussed on working with and through other organizations rather than always delivering services themselves.

However, there is a danger that a government which is purely an enabling authority could become captive of its environment. Managers in the city of Phoenix recognized this when they decided to contract out solid waste collection, but kept some internal capacity to perform the service as well. A bureaucracy of contract administrators might not understand enough about the details of a service to ask the right questions and hold the service providers truly accountable for their actions.

CONCLUSION

This paper has argued that local government has the ability to be much more innovative than it has been, but that certain fairly significant changes need to be made in its structures of governance, its modes of collective action, and its management if it is to deliver everything that it could. The other major argument is that the new view of reinventing government by making it more innovative and entrepreneurial must be approached with some care. On the one hand, it is a breath of fresh air which could improve the operation of government significantly. On the other hand, the previous section has identified some dangers in an excessive emphasis on client-centred behaviour or entrepreneurialism at the expense of a concern for the broader public interest.

1.   David Osborne and Ted Gaebler, *Reinventing Government* (Reading, Mass.: Addison-Wesley Publishing Company, 1992).

2.   This idea was set out with particular application to local government in: Ted A. Gaebler, "The Entrepreneurial Manger," in Barbara H. Moore (ed.), *The Entrepreneur in Local Government* (Washington, D.C.: International City Management Association, 1983), pp. 3-8.

3.   Rodney Brooke, *Managing the Enabling Authority* (Essex: Longman, 1989).

4.   David Osborne, *Laboratories of Democracy* (Boston: Harvard Business School Press, 1988).

5.   Rosabeth Moss Kanter, "The Organizational Climate for Innovation," in Moore (ed.), *The Entrepreneur in Local Government,* pp. 30, 39.

6.   For a review of the winners and entrants in the 1992 competition, see: *Public Sector Management,* Fall 1992, pp. 4-15.

7.   Although this could never be confirmed, it is suspected that one of the reasons that local governments are under-represented is that they are reluctant to spend the time needed to prepare a submission to blow their own horn.

8.   Susan D. Phillips, "How Ottawa Blends: Shifting Government Relationships with Interest Groups," in Frances Abele (ed.), *How Ottawa Spends: The Politics of Fragmentation 1991-92* (Ottawa: Carleton University Press, 1991), pp. 185-86.

9.   For a discussion of the need for some budget flexibility in order to innovate, see: Kanter, "The Organizational Climate for Innovation," pp. 21 and 39. See also: James L. Hetland, Jr., "Restructuring Service Delivery: The Basic Issue for Government," in Moore (ed.), *The Entrepreneur in Local Government,* p. 53.

10.   Graham Allison, *Essence of Decision* (Boston: Little, Brown, 1971).

11.   This style of provincial-municipal relations has been identified in a number of different functions. See: Allan K. McDougall, "Policing in Ontario," (unpublished Ph.D. thesis, University of Toronto, 1971); M. J. Powell, "Provincial-Local Relations in Ontario: The Case of Public

Health, 1882-1984," (unpublished Ph.D. thesis, University of Toronto, 1991); David Siegel, "Provincial-Municipal Relations in Ontario: A Case Study of Roads," (unpublished Ph.D. thesis, University of Toronto, 1983).

12. This problem is discussed in detail in the theses mentioned in note 11.

13. L. J. Sharpe, "Theories and Values of Local Government," *Political Studies,* vol. 18, no. 2 (1970), pp. 166-67.

14. David Siegel, "Disentangling Provincial-Municipal Relations in Ontario," *Public Sector Management,* Fall 1992, pp. 29-31.

15. See various editions of *Road Runner* in 1991 and 1992 published by the Ontario Good Roads Association.

16. Nasreine Canaran, "How to Cut the Gordian Knot: Provincial-Municipal Financial Entanglement," *Municipal World,* Vol. 101, no. 3 (March 1991), pp. 20-21.

17. T. J. Plunkett, *City Management in Canada: The Role of the Chief Administrative Officer* (Toronto: Institute of Public Administration of Canada, 1992), pp. 60-63.

18. Roy E. Greene, *The Profession of Local Government Management* (New York: Praeger, 1989), chaps. 2, 5.

19. The new Master's in Public Administration program at the University of Western Ontario is the first Canadian program to provide a generalist education for municipal managers. This program will be discussed in more detail later.

20. David L. Martin, *Running City Hall: Municipal Administration in America,* 2nd ed. (Tuscaloosa, Ala.: University of Alabama Press, 1990), p. 84.

21. The title chief administrative officer is more usual in Canada than city manager, although the latter term is becoming more common. There are differences in how the positions are perceived in the two countries, but these differences have more to do with the organizational culture than the title. For the purposes of this paper, the two titles can be taken as synonymous.

22. I feel compelled to use non-sexist language, although the lack of diversity in backgrounds of municipal managers is indicated by the presence of only a small number of women in senior positions.

23. For some data on the backgrounds of chief administrative officers in Ontario municipalities, see: W. George R. Vance, "The Managerial Approaches of Chief Administrative Officers," (unpublished Ph.D. thesis, University of Western Ontario, 1985), pp. 180-83.

24. For a good, general review of the challenges facing someone in this position, see: Plunkett, *City Management in Canada,* pp. 56ff.

25. These phrases are borrowed from Vance, "The Managerial Approaches of Chief Administrative Officers, pp. 221ff.

26. Vance, "The Managerial Approaches of Chief Administrative Officers," chap. 6.

27. Brooke, *Managing the Enabling Authority,* p. 8.

28. Brooke, *Managing the Enabling Authority,* chap. 2.

29. Québec, Secrétariat aux affaires régionales, *Developing Québec's Regions,* 1992, p. 17.

30. Québec, Secrétariat aux affaires régionales, *Developing Québec's Regions,* p. 35.

31. Sharpe, "Theories and Values of Local Government," p. 160.

32. Alan Norton, "Western European Local Government in Comparative Perspective," in Richard Batley and Gerry Stoker (eds.), *Local Government in Europe* (New York: St. Martin's Press, 1991), p. 27.

33. Commission on Planning and Development Reform in Ontario, *Draft Report,* December 18, 1992.

34. John Stewart and Gerry Stoker, "The 'Free Local Government' Experiments and the Program of Public Service Reform in Scandinavia," in Colin Crouch and David Marquand (eds.), *The New Centralism* (Oxford: Basil Blackwell, 1989), pp. 125-42; Petter Lodden, "The 'Free Local Government' Experiment in Norway," in Batley and Stoker (eds.), *Local Government in Europe,* pp. 198-209.

35. IMAA is a system developed by the federal government to allow departments to be exempt from certain detailed Treasury Board controls if they will accept other forms of accountability. See: Kenneth Kernaghan and David Siegel, *Public Administration in Canada,* 2nd ed. (Scarborough, Ont.: Nelson Canada, 1991), pp. 364-65.

36. Vance, "The Managerial Approaches of Chief Administrative Officers," chap. 6.

37. Osborne and Gaebler, *Reinventing Government,* pp. 76-79.

38. Gerry Stoker, "Creating a Local Government for a Post-Fordist Society: The Thatcherite Project?" in John Stewart and Gerry Stoker (eds.), *The Future of Local Government* (London: Macmillan, 1989), p. 164.

39. Eugene Lewis, *Public Entrepreneurship: Toward a Theory of Bureaucratic Political Power* (Bloomington, Ind.: Indiana University Press, 1980).

40. William W. Turner, *Hoover's FBI* (New York: Dell Publishing Co., 1970).

41. Robert A. Caro, *The Power Broker: Robert Moses and the Fall of New York* (New York: Alfred A. Knopf, 1974); Jack Newfield and Paul DuBrul, *The Abuse of Power: The Permanent Government and the Fall of New York* (New York: Penguin Books, 1978).

COMMENTS ON

DAVID SIEGEL'S PAPER

In addressing how local government administration differs from administration at other levels, David Siegel:

- proposes that provincial authorities give municipalities increased autonomy, allowing them greater freedom of action;
- suggests that associations of cities strengthen their position and target long-term objectives; and
- recommends that professional training for city managers be improved.

I generally support these orientations, although I must distance myself from some of the proposed applications.

However, before commenting on two of the three topics discussed by Siegel — first, the relationship between cities and the provincial government, and second, city management — let me say a few words about the context to help us understand the situations Siegel and I are considering.

THE CONTEXT

In their work, David Osborne and Ted Gaebler propose that governments "solve their problems" by coming out of isolation and building bridges with the society that is the very reason for their existence. I am

referring more specifically to principles such as:
- steering more than rowing;
- empowering communities rather than delivering services;
- encouraging competition rather than monopoly; and
- solving problems by leveraging the marketplace.

The very fact of having to encourage governments to re-establish links with the rest of society is truly revealing in terms of the amount of work that has yet to be done. Governments must strengthen bonds with their partners and share, even more, the philosophy behind their actions. It is impossible to create the right environment for reform without a clear understanding of the trends shaping the society that this change would affect.

What are those trends? One is the scale of government action, which differs from one society to another. According to the Organization for Economic Co-operation and Development, the combined spending of all public administrations in Canada in 1989 represented 42 percent of the gross national product (GNP), while in the United States this represented only 35 percent of GNP. If we take away defence spending, the discrepancy becomes even more significant: in Canada, public spending in the civilian area in 1989 represented 40 percent of GNP, compared to 29 percent in the US. In addition to this significant disparity, other elements must be taken into account.

For example, modernization of the Quebec government, which took place throughout the 1960s, was marked by greater integration of the public and private sectors. In fact, the "révolution tranquille" entailed more than just a reform of government structure: it led the Quebec government to play the role of a lever to rectify a weak economy. This proactive attitude has considerably changed Quebecers' perception of public administration and its institutions.

Since then, the Quebec population has consistently encouraged the use of public funds to foster economic development instruments — for example, the *Caisse de dépôt et placement,* various public or para-governmental corporations involved in developing specific sectors, the Quebec health insurance program and the Quebec stock savings plan, to name but a few.

This interventionist approach on the part of the province has led governments to sponsor compensatory actions, which have often created economic distortions. This is not only true for Quebec, but also for

Canada. To cite one example, the Canadian unemployment insurance program was designed to offset temporary loss of income due to unemployment. Over time, it became an income security program, a maternity leave program, a labour market training program, and so on.

This example reflects the complexity of all reforms, since no program can be changed without eliminating the many distortions it has generated. Therefore, no one can claim that public administration reforms, even those that appear to be sectoral, concern only public administration. All significant reforms call into question, in one way or another, the relationship between government and the public.

We must examine the impact of reforms on the quality of life of our citizens, whose environment, particularly in large cities, is often marked by social problems. In fact, large cities attract not only wealthy economic leaders, but also populations seeking integration, such as immigrants, or marginalized people, such as the unemployed and, more generally, individuals with various problems.

In Quebec, where the line between the public and private sectors is blurred, government policies have to be addressed with a holistic vision. The more we procrastinate, the more our chances for successfully implementing the appropriate reforms are compromised. Whether it be on the Canadian or the Quebec scene, we must develop a new societal framework that includes the largest possible number of social groups.

It is in the best interest of all cities that public administrations show enhanced productivity gains. Large cities also have a specific interest in ensuring that sectoral gains do not produce induced effects that would increase our marginalized population. Because the urban environment is characterized by multiple and rapid exchanges, the effects of poorly designed reforms are soon felt.

With a public debt in Canada now representing 68 percent of GNP, the debate could very well take us beyond productivity gains in the public sector. Being a better player is no longer sufficient; we need a new set of rules.

RELATIONSHIP WITH THE PROVINCIAL GOVERNMENT

Siegel has proposed that the relationship between municipalities and provincial governments be reviewed with an eye to creating greater flexibility. Given the specific context in Canada and Quebec, Montreal must go even further.

With a population of over one million, more than the population of five Canadian provinces taken individually (the four Atlantic provinces and Saskatchewan) and a budget of almost $2 billion, Montreal cannot remain indifferent to the major challenges posed by government reform, even if it is to simply anticipate the impact such reform could have on the city. While giving increased support to associations of cities, Montreal must also maintain its own relationships with the Quebec and Canadian governments.

Siegel further suggests that provincial controls and the way they are applied to municipalities be re-examined, and more importantly, that we "move away from detailed controls to the provision of more general mandates or what is called in Europe 'general competence.'"FN1 On this subject, I would like to share my views on two issues: decentralizing power to local administrations and municipal taxation.

From a local standpoint, the concentration of power in provincial and federal governments makes Canada an extremely centralized and bureaucratized country. New and more diverse needs require that we make gains on response time and that we adapt solutions to the realities. For example, we need to use the latest information and communications technologies.

I cannot envision clearly how the Canadian and Quebec governments will be capable of adapting to these new needs without further decentralizing power — especially now that it has become clear, as Siegel indicated, that innovation takes hold much more easily at the local level, with each municipality acting as a living laboratory for change.

Although we feel that the need for decentralization is evident and in several areas is a premise for change, new decentralized powers should not be transferred to municipalities without restraints. First of all, since municipalities vary in size, not all are capable of taking on new responsibilities. In some regions where there are no large centres, increased responsibility should remain with regional agencies. On the other hand, large cities can take on new responsibilities for a specific area, as Montreal has done in the areas of welfare, housing, immigration and heritage, subject to agreements approved by both levels of government.

However, governments must avoid transferring deficit-generating programs to municipalities that are no longer capable of supporting extra expenditure, and more importantly, whose source of revenue comes from property taxes — an inappropriate fiscal method of redistributing funds to social programs.

Siegel has suggested a more flexible framework for taxing municipalities. I fully agree! This is especially true since Montreal is the only major North American city which draws 85 percent of its revenue from property taxes. This is a result of the tax reform the provincial government implemented more than ten years ago to guarantee that municipalities are the prime beneficiaries of this source of taxation. This source has since been shared with the education sector.

Wealth is increasingly the result of skilled and competent human resources that are, in addition, extremely mobile. To keep this valuable workforce, governments tend to ease off on personal and corporate taxation, making up for this lost revenue through property tax transfers.

For the past three years, the government of Quebec has confirmed this trend, introducing a series of "counter tax reforms" through which it transferred specific programs to the municipalities, among them public transportation, road maintenance and police department-related costs. Such unilateral decisions go against the movement to define collectively a new framework for society.

In a recent report submitted to the Task Force on Greater Montreal established by the Quebec government, the Ville de Montréal proposed that the sharing of taxation fields be reviewed; it has also requested that it again be allowed to collect part of the consumption tax.

MANAGEMENT OF CITIES

One of Siegel's major proposals is to improve career development and training for local government managers, or Chief Administrative Officers (CAOs). Once again, I agree. For an administration to reduce response time, we need not only improved information and communications technologies but, above all, better trained human resources. Human resources, whether in the private or public sectors, represent great wealth. In this respect, for the past several years the Ville de Montréal has provided training for its managers at the *École nationale d'administration publique* (ENAP) and the *École des hautes études commerciales* (HEC), our public administration and business schools. But we have to do more.

Continuous upgrading of human-resource quality has been the

major factor contributing to the modernization of Montreal's administration. The process began in 1987 with administrative reform aimed at changing the administration into a modern, efficient public enterprise whose goal is to provide services to the population.

By reducing levels of hierarchy and decentralizing through increased delegation of power to managers who are closer to daily operations, the administration now believes it is more in tune with residents' needs and that services are more accessible. This was recognized in 1990 when the Ville de Montréal became the first Canadian public administration to receive the annual Award for Innovative Management from the Institute of Public Administration of Canada for its *Accès Montréal* offices.

The administrative reform included more than internal changes. It allowed the administration to energize its relations with its partners — following the "managing out" principle proposed by Siegel.

I want to emphasize the importance of maintaining a close relationship with partners and would like to give you an example of how the city does just that. The Ville de Montréal has contract agreements with several categories of partners, including city employees, suppliers, subcontractors, other governments and public agencies and some one thousand organizations. Of course, we can't discuss all the categories; for the time being let's look at partners in the recreational area.

For the past decade, Ville de Montréal recreational policy has encouraged partnership. As a result, the city signed agreements with 2,300 organizations involving 30,000 volunteers. Since the city assigns 1,000 employees to recreation, we estimate that for each hour an employee works, a volunteer puts in ten. It's easy to see that unless we make drastic cuts in public services, we can't revert to the old way of delivering recreational activities. In the short term, we anticipate that this trend will spread to other sectors, within or beyond our jurisdiction, where a similar approach will be followed; possible areas include care for the elderly, support to the homeless, prevention of delinquency and the fight against illiteracy.

Volunteer contributions are not new. In many areas, these contributions existed well before public services were introduced. However, if we expect volunteer contributions to be fully recognized and valued, we must include them in a broader, better defined societal framework.

Let the nature of volunteer contributions be clearly understood. Taken individually, each volunteer contribution can be explained by a need to feel useful or even by an interest in recreational activity. Whatever the motivation, from the program managers' viewpoint, volunteer work results in reduced costs. By becoming more widespread, partnership has great potential because it allows a sharing of responsibilities with administrations; this means those involved as volunteers are far from being a captive labour force.

Well rooted in our society, more so than in government, social partners will be in a position to foster public debate, question the shape of government and assure that, as Siegel underlined, the "public interest" will be well served.

Note

1. David Siegel, "Reinventing Local Government: The Promise and the Problems," this volume, p. 191.

S U M M A R Y   O F   D I S C U S S I O N

One participant asked Ted Gaebler about the process of "managing up," which David Siegel had referred to in his paper. The intervener commented that this seems to be an area where governments and bureaucracies have not performed very well. Gaebler responded that indeed this is recognized as a difficulty and noted that several business schools have devoted some of their resources to training for "managing up." Gaebler added that some of these questions relate to the possible excesses of entrepreneurship within government: contained within every solution are the seeds of its own destruction.

(Time did not permit further discussion of Siegel's paper.)

RAPPORTEUR'S COMMENTS

We've covered quite a lot of ground — and different ground — in these sessions. In making a few concluding observations, I hope to draw out some of the main themes as I saw them.

The first observation is that if we had this to do over again and were developing a title, we could probably move from the concept of "reinventing government" to "reinventing governance." I sense around the table that most people would agree with the view that the debate really needs to go beyond the structure and size of government and how it works within or is managed. Now this of course is not meant as a criticism of the book *Reinventing Government,* because it is very much concerned with the link, the relations, between government and citizens, whether they be citizens in the broadest sense of the word, or consumers of government services — clients as they are sometimes called.

We also heard, and this is part of the reason why I say that we might have used a different title, that we need to look at the broader political process — whether it be the political parties, Parliament, consultation methods and so on. Louis Bernard touched on this in his comments. As part of this broader debate, we also need to look at the links among the parts of the system of government. In this context, I think an important issue is accountability. Bill Jenkins talked about how the issue has acquired more prominence and more resonance in Britain as the system has become more complex — a near-federation as he suggested.

Another theme which came out very strongly is that we need to look at the potential for democratization as part of this reinventing of governance. Some people suggest, and Susan Phillips alluded to this, that there is a tension, almost a juxtaposition, between efficiency and democracy — even that they are totally at odds. A very interesting chapter by Bruce Doern in this year's *How Ottawa Spends*[1] actually uses those terms. He refers to the "efficiency-democracy bargain" and looks at the tension between government reform and the potential for democratization. The latter presents a real challenge, of course. It is particularly a challenge when the resources are scarce and when there is this very high level of scepticism, indeed hostility, toward government generally in the country. But this scepticism is a good reason to look even more closely at the potential for democratization.

It is plain, as we heard in the discussions, that the pressures are there for greater involvement and participation. Susan Phillips referred to this as a quasi-right, and although maybe not everyone would agree with that expression, I think it does touch on a further theme that is part of the debate.

Liora Salter used the concept of key words as a research technique for her paper. If I were to do that for this conference, I guess there is one word that would emerge. And it is not very difficult for anyone to answer which it would be: it is "change." Here I would like to take issue slightly with one of Ted Gaebler's comments. I didn't perceive a bias against change around this table. The degree of change, of course, is a question that I think will remain unanswered here. But it is fair to say that people have pointed out that there are costs, that we should be clear-sighted and that we should keep our perspective quite broad when we are looking at this change. Some of this change is inevitable. It is going to come. Diane Wilhelmy spoke about the crisis in public finance; that is going to be a pressure for change. She also reminded us that there is a risk this pressure may create a bias in reform, so there is the question of keeping one's sights on the various perspectives and objectives that Monique Jérôme-Forget enumerated in her opening remarks.

Paul Thomas gave us some evidence about certain changes that come as a result of fiscal constraint. He said in his paper that downsizing and redesign are more successful if the organization is flexible and has an external orientation. He also mentioned that there is evidence that the result may be greater control and supervision by central agencies. This of course runs against the "new managerialism," as it is sometimes called, and Sandford Borins made similar points about this.

We had quite a lot of discussion — a good lively discussion I thought —about the difference between public sector and private sector organizations. Paul Thomas referred to the public service as a loose confederacy of departments and agencies, and suggested that this will be a factor on the path to change. He also reminded us that the external environments of public organizations are more complicated and interconnected than those of private firms.

Paul Thomas also mentioned that sometimes the expressions "cultural change" and "culture" are seen as magic elixir, and I think this is quite true. People who are familiar with the Public Service 2000 process will know that those terms were very much part of the argument there. It is a moot question whether this approach is the kind of magic elixir people sometimes think it is. Francine Séguin, in some important research,[2] has documented how cultural change, whether within the private sector or the public sector, is bound to be rather slow. We heard some discussion from Paul Thomas and Ted Gaebler about the percentage of those inside who resist: the former said 30 percent and the latter said 60 percent.

Finally, there is the whole question of what is the most powerful catalyst for change. Paul Thomas suggested there are two. One is the reaction to a crisis and the other is response to new leadership. Ted Gaebler suggested and advocated very strongly that, to a large degree, change comes from within, from energy sources inside a government and from generating a sense of pride and ownership — although he mentioned, too, that this must be paired with factors in the environment. I think all of these are part of the process, the necessary process. I suppose if I have a bias to show it would be to agree with Claude Forget that unless there is a major effort at the political level, the degree of change that at least some people are thinking about is unlikely to occur.

Speaking of change, I am sure we all appreciated how Bill Jenkins brought us up to speed with the British experience. I think it is a very interesting tale, as Louis Bernard said, of not only the fact that something was done, but that so much was done in so little time — and this in a country, if I may say, not known for institutional radicalism. There has long been a lively debate in Britain about major institutional changes — a written constitution, a charter of rights, abolishing the House of Lords, electing the House of Lords, and so on. But very little has actually been acted on. Bill Jenkins calls on the British people to carry it further because he suggests that even though there has been a great deal of change, this has not been part of an overall strategy, and that if real decentralization and empowerment are to occur, there need to be changes in the machinery and the political workings of government.

This takes us back to the whole question of governance, which, from both an intellectual and practical perspective, needs to be much broader than is sometimes the case in this debate. I have had a stimulating day and I hope that participants will go away with some stimulating ideas themselves and perhaps agree that what we need to look at is reinventing governance.

1. Bruce Doern, "Efficiency-Democracy Bargains in the Reinvention of Federal Government Organization," in Susan D. Phillips (ed.), *How Ottawa Spends 1993-1994* (Ottawa: Carleton University Press, 1993), pp. 203-29.

2. Francine Séguin, "Service to the public: A major strategic change," *Canadian Public Administration,* Vol. 34, no. 3 (Autumn 1991), pp. 465-73.

Louis Bernard has occupied positions at the senior levels of the Quebec civil service as legal adviser to the Minister of Federal-Provincial Relations, Assistant Deputy Minister of Intergovernmental Affairs and head of the Premier's Office. For eight years, Mr. Bernard was Secretary General of the Executive Council, and as such was the senior civil servant in Quebec. Since 1987, Mr. Bernard has been Senior Vice-President of the Laurentian Bank where he is responsible for legal affairs, secretariat, human resources, security and internal audit.

Sandford Borins is Professor of Public Management and Director of the Centre for Public Management in the Faculty of Management at the University of Toronto. He has been a consultant to federal and provincial government departments, the Royal Commission on National Passenger Transportation and the United States National Academy of Sciences. He has written extensively on public management and recently co-authored *Political Management in Canada* with Allan Blakeney.

Ted Gaebler is President of the Gaebler Group, a division of Municipal Resource Consultants, which specializes in assisting state and local government agencies restructure existing resources and implement change through economic and organizational development. His public service includes ten years as a city manager, and ten years as an assistant city manager, in California, Oregon, Ohio, Pennsylvania and Maryland. He is the co-author of the best-selling and influential book, *Reinventing Government*. This book has caught the attention of governments and public servants in North America and Europe, where it has stimulated a debate on the way public business is conducted.

Andrew Gray is Reader in Public Accountability and Management in the Faculty of Social Sciences, University of Kent, Canterbury, England. He has written extensively on the organization and administration of British central and local government. Among his publications are *Administrative Politics in British Government* (with Bill Jenkins) and the edited volume (with Bill Jenkins and Bob Segsworth), *Budgeting, Auditing and Evaluation: Functions and Integration in Seven Governments*.

Bill Jenkins is Reader in Public Policy and Management in the Faculty of Social Sciences, University of Kent, Canterbury, England. He has written extensively on the organization and administration of British central and local government. Among his publications are *Administrative Politics in British Government* (with Andrew Gray) and the edited volume (with Andrew Gray and Bob Segsworth), *Budgeting, Auditing and Evaluation: Functions and Integration in Seven Governments.*

Monique Jérôme-Forget is President of IRPP. She was previously chairperson of Quebec's *Commission de la santé et de la sécurité du travail,* Vice-Rector of Concordia University responsible for institutional research and finance, and Assistant Deputy Minister of Health and Welfare Canada responsible for policy planning and information.

Jacques Léveillée was on leave from his position as Professor in the Department of Political Science at the Université du Québec à Montréal from 1990 to 1993. From July 1990 to February 1991 he was Coordinator of the Working Group on Government and Fiscal Decentralization at the City of Montreal. At the time of the roundtable, he was Assistant Director, Research and Intergovernmental Relations. He has written on the administration of public services and the economic and other challenges facing Montreal.

Susan Phillips is an Assistant Professor in the School of Public Administration at Carleton University. Her research interests centre on social movements and interest groups in the policy process, and she has published a number of journal articles and book chapters on these subjects. She is the current editor of *How Ottawa Spends,* the annual review of public policy and government spending published by the School of Public Administration at Carleton University.

Liora Salter is Professor at Osgoode Hall Law School and the Faculty of Environmental Studies at York University, an Associate of the Canadian Institute for Advanced Research and a Fellow of the Royal Society of Canada. She has acted as a consultant to a number of federal and provincial organizations, including the Science Council, the Canada Council and seven Royal Commissions. Liora Salter has written *Mandated Science: Science and Scientists in the Making of Standards,* co-edited

Managing Technology: A Social Science Perspective and co-authored the forthcoming *Outside the Lines: Issues in Interdisciplinary Research.*

F. Leslie Seidle is Research Director of the Governance Program of
IRPP. He was previously a senior policy adviser in the Federal-Provincial
Relations Office, Government of Canada, and Senior Research
Coordinator for the Royal Commission on Electoral Reform and Party
Financing. He is the author of articles on administrative reform, consti-
tutional reform, electoral systems and political finance.

David Siegel is Associate Professor in the Department of Politics of
Brock University and an Adjunct Associate Professor in the School of
Public Administration of Queen's University. He has served as President
of the Canadian Association of Programs in Public Administration and
on the Board of Directors of the Ontario Municipal Management
Institute. He has co-authored *Public Administration in Canada,* written
numerous book chapters and contributed articles to *Canadian Public
Administration, Optimum* and *Policy Options.*

Paul Thomas is Professor in the Department of Political Studies at
the University of Manitoba. He has advised the Royal Commission on
Financial Management and Accountability, the Royal Commission on
the Economic Union and Development Prospects for Canada and the
Royal Commission on Electoral Reform and Party Financing. He has
written extensively on federal parliamentary affairs, political parties and
public administration in Canada, and has contributed to numerous edited books and scholarly journals.